SPIRITUAL HUNGER, THE GOD-MEN
AND OTHER SERMONS
by John G. Lake

Edited by Gordon Lindsay

Published by
CHRIST FOR THE NATIONS, INC.
Dallas, Texas
The Year 1976
All Rights Reserved

Dr. John G. Lake
1870-1935

TABLE OF CONTENTS

Chapter 1
Spiritual Hunger 5

Chapter 2
The God-Men 19

Chapter 3
Christ Liveth In Me 29

Chapter 4
Sanctification of
Spirit, Soul and Body 41

Chapter 5
The Strong Man's Way to God 50

Chapter 6
The Ultimate Test of
True Christianity 62

Chapter 7
Compassion 69

Chapter 8
Fellowship With God 76

Chapter 9
The Secret of Miracles 85

Chapter 10
The Habitation of God 95

CHAPTER 1

SPIRITUAL HUNGER

"Blessed are they which do hunger and thirst after righteousness: for they shall be filled" (Matt. 5:6).

Hunger can be a good thing. It is the greatest persuader I know of. It is a marvelous power. Nations have learned that you can do almost anything with a populace until they get hungry. But when they get hungry, watch out. There is a certain spirit of desperation that accompanies hunger.

I wish we all had it spiritually. I wish we were desperately hungry for God. Wouldn't it be glorious? It would be a strange thing, if we were all desperately hungry for God, if only one or two got filled in a service.

"Blessed are they which do hunger and thirst after righteousness."

Righteousness is the rightness of God. The rightness of God in your spirit, the rightness of God in your soul, the rightness of God in your body, the rightness of God in your affairs, in your home, in your business, everywhere.

God is an all-around God. His power operates from every side. The artists paint a halo around the head of Jesus to show that there is a radiation of glory from His person. They might just as well put it around His feet or any part of His person. It is the radiant glory of the indwelling God, radiating out through the personality. There is nothing more wonderful than the indwelling of God in the human life. The most supreme example that God ever performed was His taking possession of men. By the Holy Spirit He comes in and takes possession of those who are hungry.

"Blessed are they which do hunger."

I will guarantee to you that after the crucifixion of Jesus there were 120 mighty hungry folks at Jerusalem. If they had not been exceedingly hungry they would not have gotten so gloriously filled. It was because they were hungry that they were filled.

We are sometimes inclined to think of God as mechanical, as though God just set a date for this or that event to occur. But my opinion is that one of the works of the Holy Ghost is to prepare the hearts of men in advance by putting within them a strong hunger for that event that has been promised by God until it comes to pass.

The more I study history and prophecy, the more I am convinced that when Jesus Christ was born into the world He was born in answer to a tremendous heart-cry on the part of the world. The world needed God desperately. They wanted a manifestation of God tremendously, and Jesus Christ as Deliverer and Saviour came in answer to their soul's cry.

Many look forward to the second coming of Jesus as though mechanically, on a certain date, when certain events come to pass, Jesus is going to appear. I do not see it that way. I believe there must be an overwhelming hunger for the Lord's coming in the hearts of men so that a prayer such as was never prayed in the world before for Christ to come will rise to heaven. And when it rises to heaven on the part of sufficient souls, it will take Jesus Christ off the throne and bring Him down to earth.

Daniel says he was convinced by the study of the

books of prophecy, especially that of Jeremiah, that the time had come when the Israelites should be delivered from their captivity in Babylon; the 70 years were fulfilled, but there was no deliverance. So he diligently set his face to pray it into being (Daniel 9).

If deliverance were going to come to pass mechanically on a certain date, there would not have been any necessity for Daniel to get that tremendous hunger in his soul, so that he fasted and prayed in sackcloth and ashes that deliverance might come. God's purposes come to pass when our heart and mind get the real God-cry, when the real God-prayer comes into our hearts and the real God-yearning gets hold of our nature. Something is going to happen then.

No matter what your soul may be coveting, if it becomes the supreme cry in your life, not the secondary matter, or the third or fourth, the fifth or tenth, but the supreme desire of your soul, the paramount issue—all the powers and energies of your spirit, soul and body are reaching out and crying out to God for the answer—it is going to come!

LAKE'S CRY FOR DELIVERANCE

I lived in a family which for 32 years was never without an invalid in the home. Before I was 24 years of age, we had buried four brothers and four sisters, and four other members of the family were dying—hopeless, helpless invalids. I set up my own home, married a beautiful woman, and our first son was born. In only a short time I saw the same devilish train of sickness that had followed father's family had come into mine. My wife became an invalid; my son was a sickly child. Out of it all one thing developed in my nature: a cry for deliverance. My soul cried to God for deliverance. I knew nothing about the subject of healing; notwithstanding, I was a Methodist evangelist.

But my heart was crying for deliverance; my soul had come to the place where I had given up depending on man. My father had spent a fortune on the family to no avail, as if there were no stoppage to the train of hell. And let me tell you, there is no human stoppage, because the thing is settled deep in the nature of man—too deep for any material remedy to get at it. It takes the Almighty God and the Holy Spirit and the Lord Jesus Christ to get into the depth of man's nature and find the real difficulty that is there and destroy it.

If you are away from God and your heart is longing, your soul is crying for God's deliverance, He will be on hand to deliver. You will not have to cry very long until you see that the mountains are being moved, and the angel of deliverance will be there.

I finally got to that place where my supreme heart-cry was for deliverance. Tears were shed for deliverance for three years before the healing of God came to us. I could hear the groans and cries, the wretchedness and sobs, and feel my family's desperation. My heart cried, my soul sobbed, my spirit wept tears. I wanted help. I did not know enough to call directly on God for it. Isn't it a strange thing that men do not have sense enough to call on God for physical difficulties, as well as for spiritual ones? But I did not.

But one thing matured in my heart—a real hunger. And the hunger of a man's soul must be satisfied. It is a law of God which is in the depths of the Spirit. God will answer the heart that cries; God will answer the soul that asks. Christ Jesus comes to us with divine assurance and invites us when we are hungry to pray, to believe, to take from the Lord that which our soul covets and our heart yearns for.

One day the Lord of heaven came our way, and in a little while the cloud of darkness, that midnight of hell, that curse of death, was lifted. The light of God shone into our life and into our home, just the same as it existed in other men's lives and other men's homes. We learned the truth of Jesus and were able to apply the divine power of God. We were healed of the Lord.

"Blessed are they which do hunger."

THE INCIDENT OF THE COW BREAD

Once I was out on a snowshoe trip at Sault Sainte Marie, Michigan, where they used to have four or five feet of snow. I tramped for 30 miles on my snowshoes, tired and weary. I arrived home and found my wife had gone away to visit, so I went over to my sister's home. I found they were out, too. I went into the house and began to look for something to eat. I was nearly starved. I found a big cake that looked like cornbread; it was still quite warm and it smelled good. I ate it all. I thought it was awful funny stuff, and it seemed to have lumps in it. I did not understand the combination, and I was not much of a cook. About the time I had finished it my sister and her husband came in. She said, "My, you must be tired and hungry."

I said, "I was, but I just found a corn cake and I ate the whole thing."

She said, "My goodness, John, you did not eat that!"

I said, "What was it, Irene?"

"Why, that was a kind of cow bread; we grind up cobs and all."

You see, it all depends on the degree of your hunger. Things taste mighty good to a hungry man. If you wanted to confer a peculiar blessing on men at large, it would not be to give them pie, but to make them hungry, and then everything that came their way would taste everlastingly good.

THE MIRACLE UNDER THE THORN TREE

I love to tell this story because it is the story of a hungry man. A short time after I went to South Africa and God had begun to work very marvelously in the city of Johannesburg, a butcher who lived in the suburbs was advised by his physicians that he had developed such a tubercular state that he might not live more than nine months. He wanted to make provision so that his family would be cared for after he was gone. He bought a farm and undertook to develop it so that when he died his family would have a means of existence.

One day he received a letter from friends at Johannesburg telling of the coming of what they spoke of as "the American brethren," and of the wonderful things that were taking place. They told of so-and-so, a terrible drunkard, who had been converted; of his niece who had been an invalid in a wheel chair for five years who had been healed of God; how one of his other relatives had been baptized in the Holy Ghost and was speaking in tongues; of other friends and neighbors who had been baptized and healed. He told of the powerful change that had come in the community, and all the marvels a vigorous work for God produces.

Dan Von Vuuren took the letter and crawled under an African thorn tree. He spread the letter out before God and began to discuss it with the Lord. He said, "God in heaven, if you could come to Mr. So-and-so, a drunkard, and deliver him from his sin and save his soul, and put the joy of God in him; if you could come to this niece of mine, save her soul, heal her body, and send her out to be a blessing instead of a weight and burden upon her friends. If you could come to so-and-so and they were baptized in the Holy Ghost and spoke in tongues—Lord, if you can do these things at Johannesburg, you can do something for me, too."

He knelt down, put his face to the ground, and cried to God that He would do something for him. That morning Von Vuuren was so stirred by the reading of that letter that his desire to be made whole got bigger than anything else in his consciousness. His heart reached for God, and that morning his prayer went through to heaven. God came down in his life. In ten minutes he took all the breath he wanted; the pain was gone. The tuberculosis had disappeared and he was a whole man.

But that was not all. He not only received a great physical healing, but God also had literally come in and taken possession of the man's life until he did not understand himself any more.

In telling me he said, "Brother, a new prayer from heaven was born in my spirit. I had prayed for my wife's salvation for 18 years, but I never could pray through. But that morning I prayed through. It was all done when I got to the house. She stood and looked at me for two minutes, until it dawned in her soul that I was gloriously healed of God. She never asked a question as to how it took place, but fell on her knees, threw her hands up to heaven and said, 'Pray for me, Dan; for God's sake, pray for me. I must find God today.' And God came into her soul."

Von Vuuren had eleven splendid children. The mother and he began praying, and within a week the whole household of thirteen had been baptized in the Holy Ghost. He went to his brother's farm, told of the wonder that God had done, prayed through, and in a little while nineteen families were baptized in the Holy Ghost.

REVIVAL IN THE SOUTH AFRICAN PARLIAMENT

God so filled Von Vuuren's life with His glory that one morning God said to him, "Go to Pretoria.

I am going to send you to the different members of Parliament." At executive headquarters he was admitted to the presence of Premier Louis Both. Both told me about it afterwards. Premier Both said, "Lake, I had known Von Vuuren from the time he was a boy. I had known him as a reckless, rollicking fellow. But that man came into my office and stood ten feet from my desk. I looked up and before he began to speak, I began to shake in my chair. I knelt down. I had to stick my head under the desk and cry to God. Why, he looked and talked like God. He had the majesty of God. He was superhumanly wonderful."

Von Vuuren then went to the office of the Secretary of State; then to the Secretary of the Treasury. Almost the same thing took place in each instance. For 18 days God kept him going from this one to that one—lawyers, judges, and officials in the land—until every high official in the land knew there was a God, a Christ and Saviour, and a baptism of the Holy Ghost, all because Dan Von Vuuren had really hungered after God. "Blessed are they which do hunger."

For several years before I left Africa, he went up and down the land like a burning fire. Everywhere he went sinners were saved, sick were healed, men and women were baptized in the Holy Ghost, until he set the outlying districts on fire with the power of God.

PRAYER IN FRED BOSWORTH'S HOME

I sat in Fred Bosworth's home one night before Fred thought of preaching the gospel, and listened to Lillian Thistleweight (sister-in-law of Charles Parham) tell of God and His love, His sanctifying grace and power, and what real holiness is. It was not her arguments of logic that impressed me; it was herself. It was the divine holiness that came from her soul; it was the living Spirit of God that came out of the woman's life. I sat back in the room, as far away as I could get. I was self-satisfied, doing well in the world, prosperous with all the accompaniments that go with successful life. But that night my heart became so hungry that I fell on my knees, and those who were present will tell you yet that they had never heard anybody pray as I prayed.

Bosworth said long afterward, "Lake, there is one instance that I shall always remember in your life. That was the night you prayed in my home until the rafters shook, until God came down, until the fire struck, until God came in and sanctified our hearts." All the devils in hell could not make me believe there is not a real sanctified experience of Jesus Christ, when God comes in and makes your heart pure and takes self out of your nature, and gives you divine triumph over sin and self. "Blessed are they which do hunger." Beloved, pray to get hungry.

As I talked with Lillian Thistleweight, I observed the one supreme thing in that woman's soul was the consciousness of holiness. She said, "Brother, that is what we prayed for; that is what the baptism brought to us. That is what we coveted from God."

SEYMOUR'S PRAYER FOR REVIVAL

Later Brother Parham was preaching in Texas. A black man by the name of Tom Seymour came into his meeting. Parham related his experience to Brother Tom and myself. There was a deep hunger in that black man's soul. He worked as a waiter in a restaurant to support himself while preaching to a church of his own people. He knew God as his Saviour and Sanctifier. He knew the power of God to heal. But as he listened to Parham, he became convinced of a bigger thing—the baptism of the Holy Ghost. He went on to Los Angeles without receiving it, but he said he was determined to preach all of God he knew to the people.

He said, "Before I met Parham, such a hunger to have more of God was in my heart that I prayed for five hours a day for two and a half years. I got to Los Angeles, and there the hunger was not less but more. I prayed, 'God, what can I do?' The Spirit said, 'Pray more. There are better things to be had in spiritual life, but they must be sought out with faith and prayer.' 'But Lord, I am praying five hours a day now.' I increased my hours of prayer to seven, and prayed on for a year and a half more. I prayed to God to give me what Parham preached, the real Holy Ghost and fire with tongues and love and power of God like the apostles had."

God had put such a hunger into that man's heart that when the fire of God came it glorified him. I do not believe any other man in modern times had a more wonderful deluge of God in his life than God gave to that dear fellow, and the glory and power of a real Pentecost swept the world.

That black man preached to my congregation of ten thousand people when the glory and power of God was upon his spirit, and men shook and trembled and cried to God. God was in him.

"Blessed are they which do hunger, for they shall be filled."

I wonder what we are hungering for. Have we a real divine hunger, something our soul is asking for? If you have, God will answer; God will answer. By every law of the Spirit that men know, the answer is due to come. It will come! Bless God, it will come. It will come in more ways than you ever dreamed of. God is not confined to manifesting Himself in tongues and interpretations alone.

When I was a lad, I accompanied my father on a visit to the office of John A. McCall, the great insurance man. We were taken to McCall's office in his private elevator. It was the first time I had ever been in a great office building and ridden in an elevator, and I held my breath until the thing stopped. Then we stepped into his office, the most beautiful office I ever had beheld. The rugs were so thick I was afraid I would go through the floor when I stepped on them. His desk was a marvel, pure mahogany, and on the top of his desk, inlaid in mother-of-pearl, was his name, written in script. It was so magnificent that in my boyish soul I said, "I am going to have an office just like this, and a desk like that with my name in it when I am a man."

I did not know until I was in my thirtieth year how strong that was in my nature. It almost seemed to be forgotten. I was invited to Chicago to join an association of men who were establishing a life insurance company. They said, "Lake, we want you to be manager of this association." We discussed the matter for three weeks until they came to my terms, and finally the president said, "Step into this office. I want to show you something. We have a surprise for you." I stepped into an office which was the exact duplicate of John A. McCall's office, and there in the center was a desk of pure mahogany. Instead of the name of John A. McCall, it was John G. Lake inscribed in mother-of-pearl. I had never spoken of that soul-desire to a person in the world.

There is something in the call of a soul that is creative. It brings things to pass. When the supreme desire of your heart cries out to God, all the spiritual energy of your nature and the powers of God that come to you begin to concentrate and work toward that goal. Then there comes into being that which your soul calls for by the conscious creative exercise of faith; that is the creative action of faith—you and God working out and evidencing the power of creative desire.

I am a believer in the partnership of man and God. I believe there is a fusing, a symphonizing of the soul of God and man; the two become one. Not a saved man and a glorious God. But man fused into God and God fused into man, one divine creation.

When Moses stood at the Red Sea, it was not Moses and God; it was just God. God had said, "Thou shalt be as God." Not different from God, but "Thou shalt be as God." We are continually saying, "Lord, make me a channel," leaving ourselves separated from God in our thought, and expecting God to pour His spiritual power and blessing through us. That is not the highest thing. There is a greater experience than that in God's Word. It is where you and God become one. Your whole body, your whole soul, your whole mind your whole heart, your whole spirit in the rhythm and fusion and symphony of the eternal God. One in heart, one in mind, one in soul—you and God as one.

When Moses stood at the Red Sea, he tried to back out of that relationship God was establishing and tried to throw the responsibility back on God. He was overwhelmed; it was too marvelous. Surely God must not have meant it! But God knew. When Moses began to recognize himself as an individual, and God as another, it was offensive to God. He thought he could back up and pray to God to do something for him, the way God used to do in the old relationship, but he could not do it.

The idea that Moses would want to leave that place of close fellowship with Him, that inner relationship, that divine symphony of Moses' soul and God's, was offensive to God. And God said, "Wherefore criest thou unto me?" In other words, shut up your praying.

> "But lift thou up thy rod, and stretch out thine hand over the sea, and divide it . . ." (Exod. 14:15, 16).

God did not say, "Moses, you stretch forth your hand, and I will divide the sea." He said, "Stretch out thine hand over the sea, and divide it."

God was saying, "Moses, you and I are one; stretch forth your hand and divide the sea. You have all there is of Me, and I have all there is of you. We are one and indivisible." God and man become one. The heart of man, the mind of man, the soul of man enters into God, and God into him. The divine fires of the eternal Christ, by the Holy Ghost, come from heaven, and the lightnings of Jesus flash through that life. The power of Christ invigorates, manifests and demonstrates through that relationship.

God revealed that to my soul in the days when I first went to Africa, within six weeks after my feet touched the soil, and before God had given me a white church to preach in. I said, "Lord, when you give me a church in which to preach this gospel, I will preach the highest and holiest thing God's Spirit reveals to my heart. I do not care if anybody believes it or sees it; I am going to preach the vision the Son of God puts in my soul."

He put within me the vision of the glorified Christ and the glorified Christian—not a man simply saved from sin, but a man sanctified by God's power, infilled with His Spirit, created with and in Jesus Christ. One in nature, character, and substance. And my heart began to preach it, my mouth gave the message, my soul sent forth the word, and my spirit called such that wanted to be that character of man to come to the feet of the Son of God and receive His blessing and power.

The thing that was in my soul fired Dan Von Vuuren's soul and kindled the faith of the people. Wherever it spread it set men on fire for God. But in every new experience men have to be tested and established through enduring. Some grew very weary; others never had that high vision. But they had tongues, and because they had tongues they felt equal to those who had died to themselves. They had more nerve and less experience, and they dragged the standard down. God has led them through the furnace.

Friends, we need a coming up into God. This church worldwide needs to come up into God. We have been traveling around in a circle and burying our heads in the ground. We have had our eyes on the ground, instead of up in the clouds, up at the throne. Look up to the glorified One! If you want to see His bleeding hands, look to heaven where He is to see them. Do not look to Calvary to see Him. He is the risen, glorified Son of God in heaven, with all power and all authority, with the keys of hell and death! He is the divine authority, the eternal, overcoming manifestation of God in heaven. You and the glorified Christ as one are the divine manifestation of God. Come up to the throne, dear ones. Let the throne life and the throne love and the throne power and the throne spirit and the Holy Ghost in heaven possess you, and you will be a new man in Christ Jesus. And your tread will be the march of the conqueror, your crown the crown of glory, and your power the power of God.

Two months ago the fire of God descended on my soul at Spokane and God said, "Africa and the world again." I am getting ready in my soul, not to give the old message with the old fire, but the new message with the new fire—not only to ask men to be good and go to heaven when they die, but to be God-like in character, nature, and substance and being. God is priming our souls. He is going to send forth the living waters and call by experience the new order of Knights of the Morning Star into being and action.

CHAPTER 2

THE GOD-MEN

> "Are they not all ministering spirits, sent forth to minister for them who shall be heirs of salvation? Therefore we ought to give the more earnest heed to the things which we have heard, lest at any time we should let them slip. For if the word spoken by angels was stedfast, and every transgression and disobedience received a just recompence of reward; How shall we escape, if we neglect so great salvation; which at the first began to be spoken by the Lord, and was confirmed unto us by them that heard him" (Heb. 1:14, 2:1-3).

Let us look at the word "salvation." It is the great inclusive word of the gospel. It encompasses all that God does for the soul. We have broken it down to a great extent and made it mean salvation from sin, sometimes from a single transgression. But it means much more than this. It is an all-inclusive word, including all that God does for the spirit, soul, and body of man and is applicable to each department of his nature, not only in destroying the consciousness of sin, which is purely negative, but in creating a consciousness of righteousness, which is positive. Salvation is at once destructive and creative.

Mankind has lost much in limiting this work of God to a single act, or a series of acts, instead of realizing all that God does for man. To know God's purpose for your life it is necessary to know who you are, what you are, and why you are here, the whole spirit, soul, and body being brought into complete "at-one-ment" with God.

There are some overlooked declarations in the Word of God that would enlarge man's conception of the Word and purpose of God if we would only pay attention to them. Here is one:

> "But one in a certain place testified, saying, What is man, that thou art mindful of him? or the son of man, that thou visitest him? Thou madest him a little lower than the angels . . ." (Heb. 2:6-7).

The margin of my Bible says that it means, "Thou hast made him *for a while* a little lower than the angels." Some translations read, "Thou hast made him a little lower than God." I believe it means of the same quality and substance, but limited in degree of understanding. That is my conception of this verse, and I believe it harmonizes with God's picture of man all the way through the Book.

My conviction is that the greatest transformation possible to the race is that men shall realize that instead of being enemies of God and of each other, God intends us to be gods (John 10:34). The great awakening that needs to come to all our hearts, and that has come so gradually to the world, is that there is a God-power and a soul-force in the nature of man that God is endeavoring to bring forth. He is calling forth a soul-awakening to the realization that the man within is the real man. The inner man is the real governor, the true man that Jesus said was a god.

I have been questioned on that one thing as much as any other. I want to emphasize it. One day the Pharisees challenged Jesus because He said He was the Son of God. They called Him a blasphemer. They kept the letter of the law but not the spirit of it. They had become enslaved to the mere letter and were, therefore, opposed to the broader vision of Christ.

They were so angry they picked up stones and began to stone Him. Jesus turned to them and said, quoting the words God had spoken through David, "Is it not written in your law, I said, Ye are gods?" (John 10:34).

These men were not Christians. They had not been transformed by any spiritual enlightenment as yet. They were men, as we would say, living in sin. Yet to them Jesus said, "I said, *Ye are gods.*"

If that is a fact, if these men who were sinners in the common use of the term were gods and were declared so by God Himself through the prophet, and so affirmed by Jesus, then there must have been something inherent in their nature that made them gods.

As we view the Scripture from beginning to end we see the wondrous truth that man is not a separate creation detached from God, but he is a part of God Himself. God breathed His own being, His own self into the nature and being of man and "Man became a living soul" (Gen. 2:7). God breathed into man the heavenly materiality of which God Himself is composed.

Someone might say, "I thought man was mortal." As I understand the organism of man, we have our physical body with its five sensory organs, and through these organs we are brought into contact with a certain range of activity that is purely physical.

But that is not all of man! Aside from his body, there is an inner man, a spiritual man, that inhabits and pervades the outer physical man. That is the man that came from God. The man that was breathed into the body. The man that is a part of God. That is the undying man. That is the man you cannot annihilate. That is the man who cannot destroy himself. And I do not believe it is any violation of the spirit of the Word and the truth of God to say that that is the man whom God Himself cannot destroy. Why? Because God cannot destroy Himself, and man is of the substance of God. That is what Jesus had in mind when He looked into the face of the Pharisees and said, "I said, Ye are gods."

THE OPERATION OF THE SPIRITUAL MAN

We cannot readily realize what a transformation is going to come to mankind when he realizes this fact. When man subjects that great God-man of the heart to the degradations of the desires of the outer fleshly man, how that inner man must groan.

I am sure if the Spirit of God would dispel the mist obstructing our vision and quicken our consciousness so that we moved into the realization of that one fact, life would be transformed. God never intended that the outer man of the flesh should be the governor of the great man of the soul or spirit.

One can readily see that because of the finer nature, the finer construction, the finer heavenly material of which spirit is constituted, the spiritual man has a larger range of action than the physical man. Just as the outer man receives by impression, through contact, the things that occur about him, and as these are recorded in the soul, so the greater range of action of the spirit—through the spiritual senses—permits man to touch God Himself. He is able to touch the best things in the universe and bring them back in consciousness to the soul. The apostle Paul was "caught up into paradise, and heard unspeakable words . . ." (II Cor. 12:4).

The operation of the spiritual man is identical to the operation of the physical man. Both record their facts in the soul consciousness. Consequently, when we become aware of certain things in the spirit that our spirit has recognized, it is because the spirit has recorded that consciousness of its operation in the soul. Therefore, we know it.

The subject of the God-man reduces itself largely to this: Instead of man's living in obedience to the things he receives from the fibratory action of the outer man, he realizes there is a larger life and activity within, and he begins to realize some of its powers and the duty that he owes to the inner man, that man of the heart, that God-man within. And realizing this, he refuses to permit the animal to control the spirit.

There is no individual on earth but that in some degree knows the operation of the Spirit of God. I do not believe a human being lives who has not in some degree at some time been conscious of the Spirit of God and possibly heard the voice of the Spirit or realized the operation of the Spirit upon his heart. As John said, "That was the true Light, which lighteth every man that cometh into the world" (John 1:9).

In my congregation in South Africa there was a miner who lived a vile, sinful life. One day as he was working at the mine operating his drilling machine, he became aware of an inner voice speaking to him, a voice in his spirit which said, "Go down to the stope" (which was hundreds of feet down), "and call the Austrian out." An Austrian was working all alone in one of the stopes.

In telling me about it he said, "Brother Lake, I was so busy I thought perhaps it was some freak of my mind, and I went on with my work. A little while after that the voice spoke again, and this time with more authority: 'Go down to the stope and call the Austrian out.' I was still very busy, and I did not obey, thinking possibly it was my imagination." He went on with his work until that voice spoke within him the third time in an extremely urgent manner. He said, "I knew it was the voice of the Spirit of God. I dropped everything and went to the stope. As I looked down I could see the light of a candle, so I took my candle and made a motion for him to come up. When he arrived I was not able to explain why I had called him up. But as I waited, hardly knowing what to say, the whole stope suddenly fell in."

Who was it that spoke? Who possessed the foreknowledge? Whence came the voice? It was the universal mind of God.

Even though that miner was not a Christian, and although he was not obedient to the law of God or to the law of his own being—a man who lived largely in the lusts of the flesh—yet his spirit had a conscious contact with God that day.

Perhaps you too have had this same experience. Before you were a Christian and had become obedient to the mind and will of God, was there a time in your life when the Spirit of God began to deal with you, and for the first time you were conscious that your life was not in harmony with God?

THE PURPOSE OF GOD

If these things are so, as the Word of God and the law of our being declares—that there is a larger God-man within—is there anything greater in life than to give that man a chance? What is the purpose of God in our being? Is it not all summed up in this: God's endeavor to develop in the man of the soul a conscious understanding of who he is, what his powers are, the endlessness of his existence, and all the other great things that the spirit naturally sees and feels.

The development of the soul into the likeness and stature of Christ is then the greatest element and purpose that can enter our lives. God Himself puts it first; man ought not to put it second.

Do you realize that as the light of God's truth is beginning to dawn anew on the world, the new force that has taken hold of your heart is the consciousness that God has a purpose in your life, a purpose in your being here? It is a part of the great education of the soul. It is a part of that which is necessary that mankind may go on continuously, conquering and to conquer.

I have a conviction that when the curtain is drawn on this present life, it will not be to sit down with a golden harp and sing songs all the day, though I believe that will have its place. I believe in the life to come in the new sphere, or in the condition in which we will live, we must continue developing.

The Word of God speaks of the heaven of heavens, and says that Jesus is higher than all heavens. I believe we will find that development of nature—which we have been realizing to some extent in this life—will go on and on until one day man will emerge in all senses in the likeness and understanding of God as He is.

I believe there is a time in the development of the life of the soul when it is more valuable on the other side of life than it is here. I remember one whom I loved dearly and in whom I observed this peculiar thing. For months a most wonderful process of spiritualization went on in that life, until one day as I sat at my desk I looked across into her face and observed a kind of heavenly glory all about her. I said to myself, "If that condition of spiritualization continues for a couple of months longer, there will be more of her on the other side than here, and I will miss her, for she will be gone." It was that way. One day I returned and found that during my absence her spirit had departed. She had gone to be with God.

When God has got the soul developed to the place where He can trust that soul with a larger life and a larger mission, that soul is more valuable to God on the other side than it is here. I have a conviction that that is the time and that ought to be the manner of a soul's transition into the greater life.

If that is a fact, how earnestly we should desire that everything in us points to one thing: giving the man of the heart his due chance to raise up in his own God-likeness and God-greatness. And instead of being dominated by the outer man, as a son of God in the seat of authority the outer man is obedient to the inner man. That is God's purpose. That is God's intent.

In II Corinthians 10:3-5 we see how that fact was recognized by Paul. He says, "For though we walk in the flesh, we do not war after the flesh. (For the weapons of our warfare are not carnal, but mighty through God to the pulling down of strong holds); Casting down imaginations, and every high thing that exalteth itself against the knowledge of God, and bringing into captivity every thought to the obedience of Christ."

Isn't that the exercise of the soul power? Isn't that the assertion of the spirit man, taking dominion and control in the life, bringing into captivity every power of thought and conception into obedience to Christ? For the Christ-life is the greatest life mankind has ever realized.

I was amazed recently to learn that at the present time a carload of Bibles is published for every thousand of any other book in the world. Why is this? Is it not because of the new soul awakening that is going on throughout the world? Is it not that men have come to the place of development in God-consciousness and understanding of themselves that they refuse to remain any longer in ignorance concerning the great fact of life? The Bible is God's great medium of revelation.

I can well remember when the vision of Christ

and His kingdom broke over my soul, and I began to understand myself and God. I sometimes wish I had a trumpet voice that would resound throughout this old world. I would like to tell mankind that the love of God and the things of Christ are not the things they have had painted to them. They are the great invisible, majestic forces that lift the heart into contact with God and cause man to realize that he is not an animal, but he is a king and a prince unto God.

I am an orthodox evangelist, and I have worked at my calling. I have had the privilege of helping many people to come into a consciousness of salvation. It is one thing to bring a man into a surrender of himself to God, and have him receive a conscious knowledge of and contact with God. But after that there must be the great development of a soul that causes the newborn Christian to realize what and who he is. If you want to find the real source of difficulty in the modern church, that is where you can put your finger on it. The development of the soul is neglected; man is not taught his own God-likeness and authority. Instead of his dominating the conditions by the power of God, he is dominated by them.

In the old days of Methodism, Wesley insisted that every individual who was a member of the church should have a conscious knowledge of God and be in union with Him. In establishing his church, he formed classes of twelve in which the most spiritual men were to look after their class's spiritual development and report each week the soul progress of each one. But the modern church of today has lost this to a great extent.

When an individual becomes aware of the God-man within and endeavors to let that man of the heart have some scope in life, right away he becomes conscious of a great range of spiritual life that the inner man touches. It begins to radiate through all his being. That knowledge is the source of power. That inner man, that man in union with God through whom the power of God is transmitted, who understands the mind of God, fulfills his duty to God and to himself and brings the outer man into obedience.

CHAPTER 3

CHRIST LIVETH IN ME

"Christ liveth in me" (Galatians 2:20). That is the revelation of this age. That is the discovery of the moment. That is the revolutionizing power of God in the earth, the factor that is changing the spirit of religion in the world and the character of the Christian faith. It is divine vitalization.

The world is awakening to the marvelous truth that Christ is not only in heaven, but that Christ is *in you.*

The world lived in darkness for thousands of years. There was just as much electricity in the world then as now. It is not that electricity has just come into being. It was always here. But men have discovered how to utilize it and bless themselves with it.

THE GREAT MYSTERY

Christ's indwelling in the human heart is the mystery of mysteries. Paul gave it to the Gentiles as the supreme mystery of all the revelation of God, and the finality of all wonder that he knew.

Christ has a purpose in you. Christ's purpose in you is to reveal Himself to you, through you, in you. We repeat over and over that familiar phrase, "The Church which is His Body," but if we realized the truth of it and the power of it, this world would be a different place. When the Christian church realizes that they are the tangible, living, pulsating body—flesh and bones and blood and brain of Jesus Christ—and that God is manifesting through each one every minute, and is endeavoring to accomplish His will for the world through them, not through some other body, then Christian service and responsibility will be understood.

Jesus Christ operates through you. He does not operate independently of you; He operates through you. Man and God become united. That is the divine secret of a real Christian life. It is the real union, the conscious union of man and God. There is no substitute for that relationship. You can manufacture ordinances and symbols until you become dazed with them all, but still you must find God.

There is only one reality. That reality is God. The soul of man must contact God, and unless the spirit of man is truly joined to God, there is no such thing as a real Christian manifestation. All the processes of preparation by which a soul is prepared by God for such manifestation are only preliminary processes. The final end is that man may reveal God, and that God may not only have a place of residence, but also a right of action in the body and spirit of man. Every Spirit-taught man in the world is aware of how gradually his own nature has become subjected to God and His will.

I was visiting with a gentleman who had a complaint against me. He said, "I wrote you a twenty-four-page letter, and you have not received it. If you had you would not be here." I laughed. That man has been a Christian for thirty or forty years. Always a devout man, I have spoken of him frequently to my wife and my friends as one of the most consistent Christian men I have known. Yet every once in a while we see how the human nature can rise above the spirit and spoil the beauty of the life that is revealing God.

God's purpose in us is to bring all the conditions of our being into harmony with His will and His mind. God's purpose is not to make us automatons. We see a ventriloquist operating a wooden dummy, and the dummy's lips move; it looks as though it is talking. He is just moving in obedience to another power.

God has a higher purpose than making man an automaton. God's highest is to bring out all the qualities of God in your own soul, to bring out the individuality that is in your life; not to submerge or destroy, but to change it, to energize it, to enlarge it until all your individuality and personality are of the nature and substance of God.

GOD DOES NOT ELIMINATE MAN'S PERSONALITY

Once while I was in Chicago I met a couple of old friends who invited me to dinner. At dinner the lady, who is a very frank woman, said: "Mr. Lake, I have known you so long and have had such close fellowship with you for so many years that I am able to speak perfectly frankly."

I said, "Yes, absolutely."

"Well," she said, "there is something I miss about you. For lack of words I am going to put it in Paul's words—'I bear about in my body the marks of the Lord Jesus.' You do not seem to have the marks of Jesus."

I said, "That depends on whether it is the marks or mannerisms. If you are expecting that the personality God gave me is going to be changed so that I will be another man and not myself, then you will be disappointed. If those are the kinds of marks you are looking for, you will not find them. But if you are expecting to observe a man's flesh and blood, bones, spirit, and mind indwelt by God, then you will find them. Not a machine, not an automaton, or an imitation, but a man with a clear mind and a pure heart. A son of God in nature and in essence."

What is all God's effort with the world but to bring out the real man in the image of Christ, that real man with the knowledge of God? That real man, reconstructed until his very substance is the substance of God. And when you stop to reason that to its proper conclusion, that is the only way in which Jesus Christ Himself, or God the eternal Father will ever keep from living in loneliness forever and ever.

When one stops to analyze that fact, we see that God is trying to make us in all our nature and being and habits and thought, in all the structure of our life, just as beautiful and just as real and just as clear-minded and strong as Jesus Himself. Then we understand what Christ's redemption means. It is the bringing out of Christ in you until Christ in you is the One manifest. Manifest through your eyes, just as God was manifest through the eyes of Jesus; manifest through your touch, just as God was manifest through Jesus. Not a power or a life separate from yourself, but two lives made one, two natures joined, two minds operating as one, Christ in you.

THE WOMAN AND HER RHEUMATICS

In a conference in Chicago I sat with a black woman one afternoon after the meeting. She told me of her woes and sicknesses and they were many. After a time when she had grown somewhat still, I said, "Dear mother, how long have you been a Christian?"

She replied, "Since I was a child."

Then I tried to show her that God expected a development of God and His nature and the action of God in His transforming power, through the agency of the Spirit, and that there was a process of remaking and remolding that should change her nature and dissolve the rheumatics, Bright's disease, and all the other difficulties, just as truly as long ago sin dissolved out of her soul.

After the conversation had gone on to the proper point I said, "Dear sister, anybody can see that Christ dwells in your spirit." Her eyes were lovely, delightful. "Let your mind extend just a little bit. Let your thoughts comprehend that just as Jesus dwells in your spirit and also possesses your soul, in just exactly the same way He is possessing your blood and your old rheumatic bones, and that the very same thing will happen in your bones when you realize the truth that happened in your spirit when you were converted at the altar." (She had told me how she had prayed 22 days and nights until Christ was revealed in her soul as Saviour. She seemed to want to wait 22 days and nights for God to manifest Himself in the rheumatic bones, and I was trying to get her away from it.)

She said, "Brother, lay your hands on me and pray for me, and I will be healed."

I answered, "No, I want you to get well by realizing that right now that same Christ that dwells in your spirit and your soul is in your bones and in your blood and in your brain."

Presently the old lady hopped to her feet and said, "My God, He is." She had it. Christ had been imprisoned in her soul and spirit; now He was permitted to be manifest in her body.

Brother Tom Hezmalhalch came into a black meeting in Los Angeles one day where they were talking about the baptism of the Holy Ghost. He had picked up a paper and read of these peculiar meetings, and among other things that they spoke in tongues. That was new to him. He said, "If they do, and if that is real, that is an advance in the Spirit of God beyond what is common. I am going to get it."

He went and listened as the old black Frank

Seymour taught. He was trying to develop the thought of conscious cleansing, and he used the beautiful text, "Now ye are clean through the word which I have spoken unto you" (John 15:3). That became very real to Tom. After awhile the congregation was invited to come and kneel at the altar and seek God for the baptism of the Holy Spirit. Tom later told me, "John, I got up and walked forward to that old bench with the realization in my soul of the truth of the Word the man had spoken, and that the real cleansing and Cleanser was in my heart."

He knelt and prayed for a minute or two. His soul reached up and his heart believed for the baptism of the Holy Ghost. Then he arose and took one of the front seats. One of the workers said, "Brother, don't stop praying until you are baptized in the Holy Ghost."

He replied, "Jesus told me I was baptized in the Holy Ghost."

Mr. Seymour said, "Just leave him alone. He has got it. You wait and see." A few days passed, and one day Tom said the Spirit began to surge through him, and a song of praise in tongues, an angelic voice, broke through his lips.

GET STILL AND LET GOD MOVE IN YOUR LIFE

An old preacher came into my office in South Africa and said, "Brother Lake, there is something I want to talk to you about. There used to be a very remarkable manifestation in my life. It was the manifestation of tongues and interpretation. But I have not spoken in tongues for a year. I wish you would pray for me."

I said, "No, go over and lie down and get still and let God move in your life." I was writing a letter. I went on with my writing. Presently I observed that something wanted to speak in me, and I turned my head just a little to see that the old man was speaking in tongues, and I was getting the interpretation of it as I wrote the letter.

Christians are stumbling over that fact every day. You are doubting and fearing and wondering if Christ is there. Beloved brother and sister, give Him a chance to reveal Himself. He is there. Probably because of your lack of realization your soul is closed, and He is not able to reveal Himself. You know, God is never able to reveal Himself outside of the spirit or soul. The real secret of the ministry of healing is in permitting the grace of God in your heart to flow out through your hands and your nerves into the other life. That is the real secret. And one of the greatest works God has to perform is to subject our flesh to God. Many Christians, the deepest Christians who really know God in their spirit and enjoy communion with Him, are compelled to wait until a process of spiritualization takes place in them before God can reveal Himself through them. Do not imprison Christ in you. Let Him live, let Him manifest Himself, let Him find vent through you.

MANKIND'S SUPREME NEED IS LOVE

There is one great thing that the world is needing more than anything else, and I am more convinced of it every day I live. Mankind has one supreme need, and that is the love of God. The hearts of men are dying for lack of the love of God. My sister who lives in Detroit came to Milwaukee to visit us for two or three days at a convention there. As I watched her I said, "I would like to take her along and just have her love folks." She would not need to preach to them. It is not the words you say that are going to bless them. They are in need of something greater—love. They have to receive it. Then their soul will open and there will be a divine response. Give it to them; it is the love of Christ.

You have seen people who loved someone who would not respond. If there is any hard situation in God's earth, that is it—to love someone passionately and find no response in them.

I was present at the marriage of an English friend of mine. Some years later he and his wife came to visit in our home. He was a cold type of Englishman, and his wife was a warm type. One day as they started out for a walk, I noticed the passionate yearning in her soul. If he would just say something tender, something that would gratify the craving of her nature for affection. But he seemed to be completely unconscious of her need.

I was sitting on the front porch when they returned from their walk a short time later. After the lady had gone into the house I said, "Hibbs, you are one old stiff. How is it possible that you can walk down the street with a woman like your wife and not realize that her heart is crying out for you to do something that shows you love her?"

He said, "Do you think that is the difficulty? I will go and do it now."

What is it men are seeking? What is it their hearts are asking for when they are seeking God? What is their soul crying for? Mankind is separated from God. It may not be mountains of sin between you and God. It may just be that your nature is closed and unresponsive. But when the real love-touch of God is breathed into your soul, what a transformation takes place! There is probably no more delightful thing on earth than to watch a soul praying when the light of God comes in and the life of God fills his nature, and that holy affection we seek from others finds expression in him.

That is what the Lord is asking from you, and if you want to gratify the heart of Jesus Christ, that is the only way in all the world to do it. The invitation is not, "Give me thine head." The invitation is, "My son, give me thine heart." That is an affectionate relationship, a real love union in God, a real love union with God. Think of the fineness of God's purpose. He expects that same marvelous spiritual union that is brought to pass between your soul and His own to be extended so that you embrace in that union every other soul around you.

That is what the Scripture means when it talks about being baptized in one Spirit, submerged, enveloped and enveloping in one Spirit of God.

THE CASE OF THE INSANE GIRL

While in Milwaukee recently, I went out one morning with the Rev. Fockler to make a sick call. We stepped into one of the most distracted homes I have ever been in. A strange condition had developed in one of the daughters, and the household was distressed. She had tormented that household. Nobody could get near her.

They were German people, so Brother Fockler spoke to them in German. I just sat back and watched. Presently I noticed their faces begin to relax, and the strain was gone. The girl that was apparently insane came down the stairs and stood outside the door where she could not be seen except by me. He continued to converse with the family, and as their souls softened and their faith lifted, the girl's eyes began to change.

She was moved upon by the Holy Spirit until her nature responded too, and in a little while she stepped into the room. She slipped up behind Brother Fockler's chair and stood with her hands on the back of the chair. After a while she rested one hand on his shoulder. Then after a little while she put the other hand on the other shoulder. When we left that home some 15 or 20 minutes later, there was as much difference between the attitudes of those dear souls when we came and when we left as between heaven and hell. If hell has a characteristic, it is that of distraction. If heaven has a particular characteristic, it is the presence of God, the calm of God, the love of God.

There were days when the church could club men into obedience by preaching hell to them, but that day has long since passed. The world has outgrown it.

Men are discovering there is only one way, and that is the Jesus way. Jesus did not come with a club, but with the great loving heart of the Son of God. He was "moved with compassion."

This morning I lay in bed and wrote a letter, an imaginary letter to a certain individual. I was getting ready so when I came down in the morning I could dictate the sentences that would carve him right. One of the phrases was, "You great big calf, come out of it and be a man."

As I lay there I got to thinking, "If Jesus were writing this letter, I wonder what He would write." But somehow the words would not frame themselves. My soul was not in an attitude to produce such a letter. So I came downstairs, called Edna and began to dictate. I was trying to dictate a letter in the Spirit of Jesus, but it sounded more like a lawyer. After she had it written and gave it to me to sign, I read it over and saw it was not what I wanted to write at all. I laid it aside and went in to pray a little while.

After I had been praying for twenty minutes, the telephone rang. It was the man to whom I had just dictated the letter. He wanted me to come down to the Davenport Hotel. I joined him and we had three of the best hours of fellowship together.

We boast of our development in God, we speak glowingly of our spiritual experiences, but it is only once in a while that we find ourselves in the real love of God. The greater part of the time we are in ourselves rather than in Him. This proves just one thing: that Christ has not yet secured that perfect control in our life, that subjection of our nature, that absorption of our individuality, so that He is able to impregnate it and maintain it in Himself. We recede, we draw back, we close up. We imprison our Lord.

The secret of a gospel meeting is that it assists men's hearts to open. They become receptive, and the love of God finds vent in their nature for a little while and they go away saying, "Didn't we have a good time! Wasn't that a splendid meeting!"

REACHING YOUR FAMILY THROUGH LOVE

I wonder if there is anything that could not be accomplished through the love of God? Paul says there is not. "Love never faileth." Try it on your wife; try it on your children; try it on your neighbors.

I sometimes say I believe I had the hardest boys to handle that were ever born. They were strictly like the old man. After a while I saw there was only one way under God's earth to handle them. One day I went off to pray, and I said, "Lord God, help me to love these boys regardless of what they do or say." I had to love them in some dreadful places, some awful circumstances. They tried me to the limit on that prayer. Then the other day they all happened to drop into Spokane while we were away, and in a few days I received a letter from Edna. She said, "Dad, your ears must be warm. The Lake clan got together, and we sat all night discussing you. And you would not have to apologize if you heard it."

There is only one way to tie your boys to you. There is only one way to tie your girls to you. There is only one way to be a blessing to them. But it takes so much of the grace of God, and we sometimes despair and break down.

One day I said, "God, I have prayed for these fellows until I am prayed up, and I just take the whole bunch and hand them over to you. I give the whole outfit to you. They are too much for me." And you know, my troubles somehow dissolved. They began to disappear.

Sometimes we need to comprehend the bigger love, the greater heart of God's love. It is a good thing to detach your soul. Do not hold people; do not bind people. Just cut them loose and let God's love have them. We sometimes hold people with such a grip when we pray for them that they miss the blessing. Then your humanity is exercising itself, and the Spirit is being submerged.

Let your soul relax and let the Spirit of God in you take over. There is no substitute for the love of God. You have the capacity to love. All the action of the Spirit of God has its secret there.

THE HEALING OF THE DYING WOMAN

I once stood by a dying woman who was suffering and writhing in awful agony. I had prayed again and again with no results. But this day something happened inside of me. My soul broke down, and I saw that poor woman in a new light. Before I knew it I reached out and gathered her up to my soul. In a minute I knew the real thing had taken place, and I laid her back on the pillow. In five minutes she was well. God was waiting on me, until He could give to my soul the sense of tenderness that was in the Son of God.

That is the reason His name is written in imperishable memory, and the name of Jesus Christ is the most revered name in earth or sea or sky. And I am eager to get in that category of folks who can manifest the real love of God all the time.

CHAPTER 4

SANCTIFICATION OF SPIRIT, SOUL AND BODY

> "I pray God your whole spirit and soul and body be preserved blameless unto the coming of our Lord Jesus Christ. Faithful is he that calleth you, who also will do it" (I Thes. 5:23, 24).

Most of us in our reading of the Scriptures have difficulty—and it is a perfectly natural one—of recognizing body and soul only. Man is generally spoken of as a duality of body and soul. However, the Scriptures do not recognize man as a dual being, but a triune being, like God Himself.

Therefore, the apostle says: "I pray God your whole *spirit* and *soul* and *body* be preserved blameless unto the coming of our Lord Jesus Christ."

In the common translation of our English Bible there is very little distinction made between soul and spirit. It is one of the most difficult things in the world to express in another language the common truths we teach. Paul coined seventeen distinct words in his letter to the Ephesians to express the fine distinctions of soul and spirit.

Paul declares in the book of Hebrews the possibility of divisibility of soul and spirit. He says:

> "For the word of God is quick, and powerful, and sharper than any two-edged sword, piercing even to the dividing asunder of soul and spirit, and of the joints and marrow, and is a discerner of the thoughts and intents of the heart" (Heb. 4:12).

THE SPIRIT OF MAN

Beloved, the spirit of man is that great unknown realm in the lives of most men. My judgment is that the spirit lies dormant in most men until quickened by the living Spirit of God, and until fertilized by the real Spirit of Jesus Christ. But when touched by the Spirit of God, a quickening takes place. The spirit of man comes into activity and begins to operate within him. It not only discerns things in this life, but it reaches beyond this present life and becomes that means by which we touch God Himself, and by which we know and comprehend heavenly things.

In my judgment, the spirit of man is the most amazing instrument of God there is in all the world. We have this declaration in the book of Job concerning man's spirit:

> "But there is a spirit in man: and the inspiration of the Almighty giveth them understanding" (Job 32:8).

There is a spirit in man, and the inspiration of the Almighty gives him understanding. When a soul comes to God and surrenders his life to Him, we say he is converted. And by that we mean he is changed, born again of God so that the common things which were evident in His life as a fleshly being fell away and were gone, and the spiritual life appeared in him, and in the truest sense he began his walk as a child of God.

I believe a real conversion is also the awakening of the spirit of man to the consciousness of the Fatherhood of God through Jesus Christ. In order to be aware of that consciousness of union with God, it is necessary to remove everything that hides that consciousness and dims the knowledge of God.

Sin is that peculiar thing in the life of man which dims the consciousness of man so that he cannot comprehend God. When sin is removed, the veil over the soul of man is gone and the spirit of man looks into the face of God and recognizes that God is his Father through the Lord Jesus Christ. The spirit of man ascending into union with God brings into our soul the consciousness that God is our all in all.

THE SOUL OF MAN

The soul of man is that intermediate quality between body and spirit. The soul, in other words, comprehends all the action of our mental powers, the natural mind. The soul of man is that which reaches out and takes possession of the knowledge that the spirit has attained and expresses that knowledge through the outer man. The soul of man is the governing power of the constitution of man.

I feel one of the things we need to learn is this: that the soul of man, not the spirit, has a marvelous power.

If I were to endeavor to define in terms people would understand, I would speak of the action of the soul of man as that which is commonly called the subconscious. In reading the writings of psychic authors, you will observe the actions and powers they define are not the powers of the spirit in union with God, but the action of the soul of man. The soul of man is the real ego. When the Word of God speaks of the salvation of the soul, it speaks in truly scientific language. For unless the soul, the mind of man, is redeemed from his own self into the Spirit of God, that man is in my judgment still an unredeemed man.

SANCTIFICATION OF SPIRIT, SOUL AND BODY

Sanctification is calculated to apply to the needs of all our nature; first of the spirit, second of the soul, third of the body. Over and over again I have repeated those blessed words of John Wesley as he defined sanctification: "Sanctification is possessing the mind of Christ, and all the mind of Christ."

The ultimate of entire sanctification would comprehend all the mind of Christ. Christians are usually very weak in this department of their nature. Perhaps less effort has been made by Christians to develop their minds in God than in almost anything else. We pay particular attention to one thing only, the spirit, and we do not comprehend the fact that God purposed that the things God's Spirit brings to us shall be applied in a practical manner to the needs of our present life.

I was absolutely shocked one day beyond anything my spirit has ever received. A dear lady who professes not only to live a holy life, but to possess the real baptism of the Holy Ghost, and who discusses the subject a great deal, was guilty of saying one of the vilest things I ever heard concerning another person. I said in my own soul, "That individual has not even discerned the outer fringes of what sanctification by the Spirit of God means." I do not believe there is any evidence of sanctification in that life. Certainly a mind that could repeat such a thing gives evidence of only a very superficial knowledge of God.

It shows us that people are depending upon the fact that in their spirit they know God, that they have been saved from sin and are going to heaven when they die; but they are living like the devil and talking like the devil in this present life. It is an abomination. It shows a tremendous degree of ignorance. It shows that that individual does not comprehend the first principles of the breadth of salvation as Jesus taught it to the world—a holy mind, a sanctified spirit.

But here is the hope, here is the strength, herein is the power of the gospel of Jesus Christ—that the power of God unto salvation, applied to the mind of man, sanctifies the soul of man and makes the mind of man like the mind of Christ. Who could imagine from the lips of Jesus an unholy suggestion that would jar the spirit of another? The mind could not conceive of such a thing.

SANCTIFICATION OF THE MIND

One Sunday afternoon I preached in a new theater, and I never preached under such trying conditions in all my life. There was an atmosphere there that one could recognize was the effect of the minds who inhabit that place. It seemed the whole place was impregnated with that spirit and it took a long time for my spirit to overcome it so I could speak out with freedom.

In our home, in our office, wherever we are, we leave the impress of our thoughts there. If our thoughts are pure and holy, like Christ, people will walk into that atmosphere and instantly discover it.

Not long ago a brother walked into our healing rooms, and he said to me afterwards: "When I came through the outside door I felt it." He knew God and recognized the power of God. The sanctified mind leaves the balm of the holy presence and a holy thought wherever it goes. The unsanctified mind leaves the sting and the stain of unholiness.

If there is any particular area where as a rule Christians are weak, it is in the consecration of their minds. Christians seem to feel as if they are not to exercise any control over the mind, so it seems to run at random, just like the mind of the world. Real Christianity is marked by the pureness, the holiness of the thoughts of man; and if the kind of Christianity you have does not produce in your mind real holiness, real purity, real sweetness, real truth, then it is a poor brand. Change it right away.

There is relief for the unsanctified mind. Submit your mind to the Lord Jesus Christ to be remolded by the Holy Spirit, so that it becomes the pure channel of a holy nature.

Surely, we who profess to know the living God, who profess to live in union with Him, ought to present to the world that attitude and holiness of mind which needs no recommendation. People know it; they feel it. They know it is the mind of Christ.

THE EFFECT OF THE MIND ON THE PERSON

Do you know that the sins of vileness in men's lives originate in the mind? A man's life will be of the character of his thoughts. If he thinks evil, he will be evil. If he thinks holy, he will be holy. His outward life will be as the inner impulse is.

Jesus said:

> "For from within, out of the heart of men, proceed evil thoughts, adulteries, fornications, murders, thefts, covetousness, wickedness, deceit, lasciviousness, an evil eye, blasphemy, pride, foolishness: All these evil things come from within, and defile the man" (Mark 7:21-23).

The Jews were troubled because Jesus and the disciples were eating and drinking from dishes which had not been ceremonially cleansed. So Jesus was trying to teach the great lesson of the inner life. He said, "Out of the heart come evil things." That which goes into the mouth cannot defile a man.

Our minds need to be stayed in Christ, kept by the power of God, infilled with the Holy Spirit of Christ, so that we reflect His beauty and show forth His love. We should manifest His sweetness and evidence His power.

Isn't it marvelous to realize that mankind can receive into his nature the power and Spirit of the living Christ, which contains the purging power to drive forth from his being every particle of evil, every sensuous thing in his thought and nature, so that the man becomes what Jesus was?

The inflow of holy life into our bodies must produce holiness in the body just as it does in the soul. We cannot even think beautiful thoughts, we cannot think holy thoughts, without their leaving an impression in our nature, in our very flesh.

ST. FRANCIS OF ASSISI

When St. Francis of Assisi was about to die, he said to his friends, "When I am dead you can open my body, and you will observe the cross of Christ imprinted on the flesh of my heart." All through his long life as a holy man of God he had contemplated the cross of Christ, so that he had become confident that the very impression of the cross was made in the flesh of his heart. His body was opened after his death and this was found to be true. This fact is certified by the best authorities.

That same heavenly power in us dissolves disease and restores diseased tissues. Our flesh is purged by the divine power being transmitted from our spirit through our soul into our body.

When we contemplate the Lord Jesus on the Mount of Transfiguration and think of the radiant glory that came through His flesh, not just the illumination of His Spirit, but the holy glory emanating through His flesh until He became white and glistening, until His face shone as the light, we begin to understand the transfiguring power of heaven.

It is that radiant purity of God that my soul covets. It is that radiant power, evidenced in the pureness of my spirit, my mind, and my very flesh that I long for.

THE IMPURITY OF DISEASE

When something impure of the character of disease appears on your flesh and mine, and we feel we are being soiled by an unholy touch, in the name of Jesus our spirit reaches up and rebukes that devilish condition. By the Spirit of the living God we stand, believing that the Holy Spirit of God will flow through the spirit, flow through the soul, through the flesh and remedy and heal that difficulty.

An old Baptist brother came to see me about his wife. As I sat reasoning with him I said, "Brother, both sin and sickness are impure. One is the evidence of an impure mind; the other is the evidence of an impure body. And the salvation of Jesus was intended to make man pure in spirit, soul and body."

> ". . . I pray God your whole spirit and soul and body be preserved blameless unto the coming of our Lord Jesus Christ. Faithful is he that calleth you, who also will do it" (I Thes. 5:23, 24).

There is a stream of life that God permits to flow from your nature and mine to all men everywhere. That blessed stream will be either sweet and pure as the stream that flows from the throne of God, or it will be soiled and fouled, according to the condition of our nature. And the value of the precious blood of Jesus Christ to you and me is that through it that lifestream that flows from us may be made holy—that same holy, living stream that causes the tree of life to bloom.

Of all the pictures the Word of God contains, the one described in Revelation 22:1 is the most beautiful.

> "And he showed me a pure river of water of life, clear as crystal, proceeding out of the throne of God and of the Lamb."

If your life has not been satisfactory, if you have not recognized the holy character that Christ expects from a real Christian, then this call of the Spirit comes to your soul. The Spirit and the Bride say come. Come up, come into the real life, the life hid with Christ in God.

". . . I . . . shall be in him a well of water springing up into everlasting life" (John 4:14).

CHAPTER 5

THE STRONG MAN'S WAY TO GOD

Musicians talk of an ultimate note. It is a note not found on any keyboard. It is a peculiar note. A man sits down to tune a piano. He has no guide to the proper key; yet he has an inner guide. That guide is the note that he has in his soul. And the nearer he can bring his instrument into harmony with the note in his soul, the nearer he has attained perfection.

There is an ultimate note in the heart of the Christian. It is the note of conscious victory through Jesus Christ. The nearer our life is tuned to that note of conscious victory, the greater the victory that will be evidenced in our life.

In my ministry in South Africa I met a young lady, one of the most beautiful souls I have ever known. One of the remarkable developments in her life after her baptism in the Spirit was that the Spirit of God would come powerfully upon her on occasions, and at such times she would sit down at the piano and translate the music that her soul heard. Other times the Spirit would come upon her so powerfully that she would be caused to sing the heavenly music in some angelic language. God gave her the gift of interpretation so that quite frequently when the Spirit would come upon her, she would resing the song in English, or Dutch as the case might be.

Her father and mother were both musicians.

They soon learned that when the Spirit thus came upon her, they could record the music. The father would stand at one side and take down the words of the song as she sang them, while the mother stood at the other side and recorded the music as she played the music on the instrument. In this way a great deal of that music was preserved.

Some years later Clara Butts, the great English prima donna, came to Africa. She was singing at the great Wanderer's Hall in Johannesburg, and one evening after the concert, while being entertained at the hotel, I was introduced to her. She said to me, "Mr. Lake, I have been anxious to meet you, for I have heard that among your people is a remarkable woman who receives music in the Spirit, apparently of a different realm from ours."

I said, "Yes, that is a fact."

She inquired if it would be possible to meet her, and so a meeting was arranged. One evening we went to her hotel, and as we sat down, Clara Butts said to the young lady, "I wish you would sit down and play some of the music I have heard about." She did not understand that such music came only at such times as the Spirit came powerfully upon the woman. However, the young lady sat down at the piano.

I said to the company, "Let us bow our heads in prayer," and as we did and waited, presently the Spirit of God descended upon her, and then there poured through her soul some of the wondrous, beautiful, heavenly music. I waited to note the effect upon the group. When the song was finished, I looked especially at Clara Butts, who was weeping silently. She rose to her feet, and coming forward to the piano she reached out her hands, saying, "Young lady, that music belongs to a world that my soul knows little about, and I pray every day of my life that God may permit me to enter. In that realm is the ultimate which my soul sometimes hears, but which I have never been able to touch."

THE ULTIMATE NOTE

Beloved, in the Christian life, in the heart of God, there is an ultimate note—that note which is so fine and sweet and true and pure and good that it causes all our nature to respond to it and rejoices the soul with a joy unspeakable.

All down through the ages some have touched God and heard the ultimate note. I believe as David sat on the mountainside as a boy, caring for his father's sheep, God by the Spirit taught him the power and blessing of that ultimate note. At times his soul ascended unto God, and many of the psalms of David are the real soul notes of that blessed expression of heavenly music and heaven consciousness which came into the soul of the shepherd boy.

Mary, the mother of Jesus, understood that note. I remember when I was a young man in a Methodist Bible class which I taught, we were discussing the subject of the Magnificat—that glorified expression that burst from the soul of Mary as she met Elizabeth, when the Spirit came upon her and revealed to her cousin that she was to be the mother of Jesus. In our worldly wisdom we decided of course that the Jewish women of necessity must have been educated to compose such beautiful poetry spontaneously.

Later as I saw the Spirit of God descend upon a soul, and the soul break forth into a song of God, the song of the angels, in a note so high and sweet and pure and clear as no human voice ever had produced, I understood the marvel that was taking place in the soul of Mary when she broke forth into the heavenly expression of that holy song:

"My soul doth magnify the Lord, and my spirit hath rejoiced in God my Saviour" (Luke 1:46, 47).

It was the Spirit of the Lord. Her spirit had ascended into the heavenlies. Her spirit had touched heaven's note. Her spirit was receiving and reproducing the song of joy that she heard, possibly from the angels or perhaps intuitively from the heart of God.

There is a Christianity that has that high note in it. Indeed, real Christianity is in that high note of God, that thing of heaven that is not of earth and is not natural. It is the note of the heavens. It comes to the earth. It fills the soul of man. Man's soul rises into the heaven to touch God, and in touching God receives that glorified expression and experience into his own soul, and it is reproduced in his own life and nature.

There is a victory in God, the victory that characterizes the common walk of the dedicated Christian. It is a strong man's salvation. The soul who receives that heavenly touch does not have to be told by man. He knows by the Spirit that God has enlightened his heart, filled his soul, and caused his very being to radiate with God's glory and presence.

The hunger of my soul for many a day has been that I might be able to so present that high true note of God that the souls of men would rise up in God to a place of power, purity, and strength, where the character and presence of God might be evidenced in them. There is a purity of heaven so high, so holy, so pure, so sweet that it makes the life of the possessor radiant with the glory and praise of God.

Many have said that the cross of Christ was not a heroic thing, but I want to tell you that the cross of Jesus Christ has put more heroism in the souls of men than any other event in human history. Men who realized the real spirit of His holy sacrifice have lived and rejoiced and died, believing in the living God. They manifested to mankind that same measure of sacrifice, and endured all that human beings could endure. And when endurance was no longer possible, they passed on to be with God, leaving behind the evidence of a consecration deep, true, and good, like the Son of God Himself.

CHRISTIANITY NOT DESIGNED FOR WEAKLINGS

We see the note that was in the soul of Paul, and which characterized his message, when he made the splendid declaration in Romans 1:16:

> "For I am not ashamed of the gospel of Christ: for it is the power of God unto salvation to every one that believeth: to the Jew first, and also to the Greek."

We see the note that touched the souls of men, the note that rang down through the centuries, and which rings in your heart and mine today. Christianity never was designed by God to make a lot of weaklings. It was designed to bring forth a race of men who were bold, strong, pure, and good. The greatest and strongest and noblest is always the humblest.

The beautiful thing in the gospel is that it eliminates from the life of man that which is of himself and is natural, fleshly, and earthly. It brings forth the beauteous things within the soul of man, the unselfishness, the life of purity, the peace, the strength, and the power of the Son of God.

How beautiful it is to have the privilege of looking into the face of one whose nature has been thus refined by the Spirit of the Living God within.

How beautiful it is when we look into the soul of one whom we realize God has purged by the blood of Christ, and cleansed his nature and empowered it by His Spirit until the very characteristics of the life and attitudes of the mind of Christ are manifest and evident in him to the glory of God.

Christianity by the grace of God is calculated to take the weak and fallen, the erring and dying, and by applying the grace and power of God through the soul of man to the need of the individual, lift him up to the "Lamb of God which taketh away the sin of the world."

> "Down in the human heart,
> Crushed by the tempter,
> Feelings lie buried
> That grace can restore.
> Touched by a loving heart,
> Wakened by kindness,
> Chords that were broken
> Will vibrate once more."

I care not how crushed the soul, how bestialized the nature; I care not how sensual a person may be. If touched by the Spirit of the living God, he will shed that which is earthly and sensual and give forth once again the pure note of the living God, heaven's high message, heaven's triumphant song, heaven's high note of living praise to the living God.

God is endeavoring by His Spirit in these days to exalt the souls of men into that high place, that holy life, that heavenly state whereby men walk day by day, hour by hour in the heavenly consciousness of the presence of Christ.

And the presence of Christ in the souls of men can only produce the purity that is in Him. Purity is of God. Purity is of the nature of Christ. Purity is heaven's instinct, filling the soul of man, making him in His nature like the Son of God. Upon that purified soul there comes from God that blessed measure of the Holy Spirit, not only purifying the nature, but empowering him by the Spirit so the activities of God, the gift of His mind, the power of His Spirit is evident by the grace of God in that man's soul. He is lifted by the grace of God into that place of holy and heavenly dominion in the consciousness of which Jesus lived and moved and accomplished the will of God always.

THE CREATIVE POWER OF GOD IN MAN

Jesus was not bowed and overcome by conditions and circumstances about Him. He realized that the soul of man is a creative power, that it is the nature of every man to protect, accumulate, and possess, as sons of God, that through the creative faculty of his soul the desires of his heart might be brought to pass.

That is the reason God dared to talk as He did to Moses. That is the reason God dared to rebuke a man when he stopped to pray. That is the reason God said, "Wherefore criest thou unto me?. . . Lift thou up thy rod, and stretch out thine hand over the sea, and divide it" (Exod. 14:15, 16).

Your soul will never demonstrate the power of God in any appreciable degree until it conceives and understands the real vision of Christ. He knew that through His union with the living God His soul became the creative power through which He took possession of the power of God and applied it to the needs of His own soul, and the needs of other lives.

THE MINISTRY OF THE SPIRIT AMONG METHODISTS

As a boy I received my religious training in a little Methodist class meeting. I wish there were some old-time Methodist class meetings in these modern days—the kind that had the power of God where people could open their hearts and tell of their temptations and their trials and victories, and receive counsel from one who guided the class. To such a meeting I owe a great deal of the soul development which God has brought forth in my life.

In one of these class meetings one day, as I sat listening to the testimonies, I observed that there was a kind of weakening trend. People were saying, "I am having such a hard time." "I am feeling the temptations of the world so much." I was not able at that time to tell people the way out of their difficulties. I was only a young Christian.

When they got through, the old gray-haired class leader said, "Brethren, the reason we are feeling the temptations so much, the reason there is a lack of the sense of victory, is that we are too far away from the Son of God. Our souls have descended. They are not in the high place where Christ is. Let our souls ascend, and when they ascend into the realm of Christ, we will have a new note; it will be a note of victory."

HOW VICTORY COMES

Beloved, that is the difficulty with us all. We have come down out of the heavenlies into the natural, and we are trying to live a heavenly life in the natural state. We are over-burdened by the weights and cares of the flesh and life all about us. But there is deliverance. There is victory. There is a place in God where the flesh no longer comes under bondage, where, by the grace of God, every sensuous state of the human nature is brought into subjection to the living God. There is a place in God where Christ reigns in and glorifies the very activities of a man's nature, making him sweet, pure, clean, good and true.

I call on you today, by the grace of God, to that high life, to that holy walk. I challenge you to that life in God where the grace and spirit and power of God permeate your whole being—where not only your whole being is in subjection, but it flows from your nature as a holy stream of heavenly life to bless other souls everywhere by the grace of God. That is how victory comes.

There was a period in my life when God lifted my soul to a wondrous place of divine power. Indeed, I say in all humility that I believe God gave me such an anointing of power as has seldom been manifested in modern life. That anointing remained with me for a period of eight months. One of the evidences of the power of God at that period was that God gave me such a consciousness of dominion to cast out evil spirits that the insane were brought from all quarters of the land. In many instances as I approached them the Spirit of Christ would rise up in me in such dominion that when I got to them I could take hold of them, and looking into their faces, would realize God had given me power to cast out the evil spirits. Hundreds of times the insane were instantly healed right on the spot.

I have been a student all my life; not just a student of letters, but of the things of the soul. I noted that when this consciousness of heavenly dominion rested upon my life, one thing stood uppermost in all my consciousness. That was the vision of the triumphant Christ, the Son of God, as pictured by John in the first chapter of Revelation, where He stands forth in the mighty dignity of an overcomer, declaring, "I am he that liveth, and was dead; and behold, I am alive forevermore, Amen; and have the keys of hell and of death" (Rev. 1:18).

I am glad God has permitted man, even at intervals, to rise into that place of dominion in God, for it demonstrates the purposes of God. It demonstrates that He purposes that we should rise into the high place not only at intervals, but this should be the normal life of the Christian who is joined to God.

Christianity need not be apologized for. Christianity was the conscious life and power of the living God, transmitted into the nature of man until man's nature is transformed by the living touch. The very spirit, soul, and being are energized and filled by His life. Thus you become indeed as Christ intended, a veritable likeness of Him.

THE ULTIMATE NOTE IN GOD'S PLAN

That startles some people. But the ultimate note of the gospel of Jesus Christ and the ultimate of the redemption of the Son of God is to reproduce and make every man—bound by sin and held by sensuousness and enslaved by the flesh—like Himself in deed and in truth, sons of God. Not sons of God on a lower order, but sons of God as Jesus was.

Paul declares, "He gave some, apostles; and some, prophets; and some, evangelists; and some, pastors and teachers . . ." Why? "Till we all come . . . unto a perfect man, unto the measure of the stature of the fulness of Christ" (Eph. 4:11-13). Not a limited life, but an unlimited life. The idea of God was that every man should be transformed into Christ's perfect image by his being joined to Him by the Holy Spirit. Christ within and Christ without. Christ in your spirit, Christ in your soul, and Christ in your body. Not only living His life, but performing His works by the grace of God. That is the gospel of the Son of God. That is the thing Paul was not ashamed of. He said, "For I am not ashamed of the gospel of Christ: for it is the power of God unto salvation to everyone that believeth; to the Jew first, and also to the Greek" (Rom. 1:16).

DEVELOPMENT OF CHRISTIAN CONSCIOUSNESS

If anyone wants to analyze the development that has come into Christian consciousness during the last 200 years, all they have to do is to follow the preaching of the great evangelists who have moved the world. Think of Jonathan Edwards, who thundered the terrors of God and nearness of hell until men grasped their seats and hung on to them, fearing they were falling into hell itself. Men were moved by fear to escape damnation. Naturally, anyone wanted to keep out of hell. But he might not have had any idea of the real meaning of Christianity.

After a while others went a step further, and we note the ascending consciousness. They said, "No, saving yourself from hell and punishment is not the ideal of the gospel. The ideal is to get saved in order to go to heaven when you die." I have always wanted to weep when I heard men pleading with others to become Christians so they will go to heaven when they die. Is there no appeal outside of something absolutely selfish?

Christianity was unselfishness itself. It had no consideration for individual selfishness. The only ideal worthy of a Christian is that you and I might demonstrate to mankind one holy, beautiful thing of which the world is deficient: a knowledge of God. So Jesus said, "Unto all righteousness" and He wrote it on the souls of men, branded it on their consciences and stamped it on their hearts until the world began to realize the ideal that was in the soul of Jesus. That is Christianity, and that only is Christianity, for that was the consecration of Christ Himself.

CHAPTER 6

THE ULTIMATE TEST OF TRUE CHRISTIANITY

The test of the Spirit, and the only test of the Spirit Jesus ever gave, is the ultimate and final test. He said. "Ye shall know them by their fruits. Do men gather grapes of thorns, or figs of thistles?" (Matt. 7:16).

If you want to test whether this present outpouring of the Spirit of God is the real, pure baptism of the Holy Ghost or not, test it by the fruits that it produces. If it is producing in the world, as we believe it is, a consciousness of God so high, so pure, so true, so like Christ, then it is the Holy Ghost Himself. No other test is of any value whatever.

The ultimate test to your own soul of the value of a thing that you have in your heart is the common test which Jesus gave, "Ye shall know them by their fruits. Do men gather grapes of thorns, or figs of thistles?"

Men tell us in these days that sin is what you think it is. Well, it is not. Sin is what God thinks it is. You might think according to your own conscience, but God thinks according to His. God thinks in accordance with the heavenly purity of His own nature. Man thinks in accordance with that degree of purity that his soul realizes. But the ultimate note is in God.

When men rise up in their souls' aspiration to the place of God's thought, then the character of Jesus

Christ will be evident in their life, the sweetness of His nature, the holiness of His character, the beauty of the crowning glory that not only overshadowed Him, but that radiated from Him. And the real life of the Christian is the inner life, the life of the soul.

"For out of the heart," said Jesus, "proceed evil thoughts, murders, adulteries, fornications, thefts, false witness, blasphemies" (Matt. 15:19). These are the things common to the flesh of man. Out of the soul of man, likewise, proceeds by the same law the beauty, virtue, peace, power, and truth of Jesus, as the soul knows it.

He whose soul is joined to Christ may now, today, this hour, shed forth as a benediction upon the world the glory and blessing and peace and power of God, even as Jesus shed it forth to all men to the praise of God.

THE EARTHLY AND HEAVENLY MATERIALITY

One of the most difficult things to make people understand is that the Spirit of God is a tangible substance; it is the essence of God's own being.

We are composed of an earthly materiality; that is, our bodies are largely a composition of water and earth. This may sound a little crude, but the actual composition of a human being is about sixteen buckets of water and one bucket of earth. I am glad there is one bucketful of good mud in us! Water is a composition of gases, so you can see how much gas there is in mankind. But we are not all gas.

The composition of the personality of God, for God has a personality and a being and is a substance, is different from man's. Spirit is a substance. All heavenly things are of spiritual substance. The bodies of the angels are of some substance. They are not the same character of materiality as our own, for ours is an earthly materiality, but the composition of heavenly things is of a heavenly materiality. In other words, heavenly materiality is Spirit. The Word says, "God is a Spirit: and they that worship him must worship him in spirit and in truth" (John 4:24).

The spirit of a man must contact and know the real spirit of God. We do not know God with our flesh, with our hands or with our brains. We know God with our spirit. The knowledge of God that our spirit attains may be conveyed to us through the medium of our mind. The effect of God in our body comes through the medium of the spirit of man, through the mind of man into the body of man.

There is a quickening by the Spirit of God so that a man's body, a man's soul or mind, and a man's spirit become blessed, pervaded and filled with the presence of God Himself in us. The Word of God is wonderfully clear along these lines. "Thou wilt keep him in perfect peace, whose mind is stayed on thee . . ." Why? "Because he trusteth in thee" (Isa. 26:3). That is the peace that a Christian knows whose mind rests in God in perfect trust.

The Word of God says also that our flesh shall rejoice. Not our mind, but our very flesh shall rejoice. The presence of God is to be a living presence, not only in the spirit of man, nor in the mind of man alone, but also in the flesh of man, so that God is known in all the areas of his life. We know God in our very flesh; we know God in our mind; we know God in our spirit.

The medium by which God undertakes to bless the world is through the transmission of Himself. The Spirit of God is His own substance, the substance of His being, the very nature and quality of the presence and nature of God. Consequently, when we speak of the Spirit of God being transmitted to man, we are not talking about an influence, either spiritual or mental. We are talking about the transmission of the living substance and being of God into your being and into mine. Not a mental effect, but a living substance, the living being and actual life transmitted, imparted, coming from God into your being.

That is the secret of the abundant life of which Jesus spoke. He said, ". . . I am come that they might have life, and that they might have it more abundantly" (John 10:10). The reason we have the more abundant life is that, receiving God into our being, all the springs of our being are quickened by His living presence. Consequently when we receive God we live life in a fuller measure. We live life with a greater energy because we become the recipients of the energy of the living God in addition to our normal energy, by receiving His being, His nature, His life into ours.

THE RADIATING GLORY OF TRANSFIGURATION

The tremendous capacity of the human being to receive God is demonstrated by some of the incidents in the Word of God. The most remarkable in the Scriptures is the transfiguration of Jesus Himself, when the Spirit of God came upon Him so powerfully that it radiated from His being until His clothes became white and glistening, and His face shown as the light.

One must be the recipient of the light, glory and power of God before he can manifest it. Jesus demonstrated these two facts: the marvelous capacity of the nature of man to receive God into his being, and the marvelous capacity of the nature of man to reveal God. In the glory shining through His clothes, in the glistening of the glory of God upon His countenance, He demonstrated man's capacity to reveal God.

THE SPIRIT OF GOD IN HANDKERCHIEFS AND CLOTHS

The human being is the most marvelous and wonderful instrument of all the creation of God in its capacity to receive and reveal God. Paul received so much of God into his being that when men brought him their handkerchiefs and women brought him their aprons, and he took them into his hands, the handkerchiefs and aprons became impregnated with that living Spirit of God. When they were carried to one who was sick or possessed of devils, the Word says when they laid the handkerchiefs or aprons on them the Spirit of the living God passed from the handkerchief or apron into the sick, and the sick were healed and the devils were cast out.

People have been so in the habit of putting Jesus in a class by Himself that they have failed to recognize that He has made provision for the same living Spirit of God that dwelt in His own life, and of which He Himself was a living manifestation, to inhabit your being and mind, just as it inhabited the being of Jesus or Paul.

The story of the woman who touched the hem of Jesus' garment is a familiar one. Knowing how His whole being radiated that wondrous, blessed life of God of which He Himself was the living manifestation, she said within herself, "If I may but touch His garment," and as she did so there flowed into her body the quickening lifestream. She felt in her body that she was made whole of that plague.

Conscious that something had flowed from Him, Jesus asked, "Who touched my clothes?"

His disciples replied, "Thou seest the multitude thronging thee, and sayest thou, Who touched me?" (Mark 5:30, 31). But Jesus knew that someone had "touched" Him with a touch of faith, for "virtue had gone out of him." The Greek word used here for virtue means life, or the substance of His being—the quickening, living power of God, the very nature and being of God.

If I transmit to another the virtue of my life, I simply transmit to another the life-power that is in me. The life of God that flows through me is transmitted to another. And so it was with Jesus.

The fact that people brought handkerchiefs and aprons to Paul, and they became impregnated with the Spirit of God and the people were healed when they touched them, is a demonstration in itself that any material substance can become impregnated with the same living Spirit of God.

DIVINE POWER IN GOSPEL PAPERS

In my church in South Africa we published a paper in lots of ten thousand. We had the publishers send them to the tabernacle, and there we laid them out in packages of one or two hundred all around the front of the platform. At the evening service I would call certain ones of the congregation that I knew to be in contact with the living God to come and kneel and lay their hands on those packages of papers. Then we asked God that not only would the words in the paper be a blessing to those who received them, and that the message of Christ should come through the words printed on the paper, but we also asked God to make the very substance of the paper itself become filled with the Spirit of God. In the files in my tabernacle are thousands of letters from all parts of the world from people telling me that when they received our paper, the Spirit came upon them and they were healed. Or when they received the paper the joy of God came into their heart. Or they received the paper and were saved.

One woman wrote from South America saying, "I received your paper. When I received it into my hands my body began to vibrate so I could hardly sit on the chair, and I did not understand it. I laid the paper down, and after a while I took it up again; as soon as I had it in my hands I shook again. I laid it down and took it in my hands a third time; presently the Spirit of God came upon me so powerfully that I was baptized in the Holy Ghost."

This quality of the Spirit confuses the philosophers. It shows the clearest distinction which characterizes the real religion of Jesus Christ, and sets it apart from all other religions and all other ministries.

The ministry of the Christian is the ministry of the Spirit. He not only ministers words to another, but he ministers the Spirit of God. It is the Spirit of God that inhabits the words, that speaks to the spirit of another and reveals Christ in and through him.

CHAPTER 7

COMPASSION

What is the greatest blessing or revelation of the Spirit of God? I believe the greatest thing is that Jesus showed the world how to exercise compassion for one another. The law of Moses that preceded Jesus was exacting in its demands, as all law is. That is the nature of law. And Jesus undertook to reveal the Father-heart of God to the world. The greatest movement in the soul of God Himself was that movement of compassion for a needy world. It was so great that the Word says, "For God so loved the world, that he gave his only begotten Son, that whosoever believeth in him should not perish, but have everlasting life" (John 3:16).

We are inclined to think sometimes that God is careless about the world. Not so. "For God sent not his Son into the world to condemn the world; but that the world through him might be saved" (John 3:17).

When the multitude had followed Jesus into the wilderness, He was moved with compassion for them, for they were like sheep without a shepherd. The disciples said, "Now Lord, let us send them away."

Jesus understood men's humanity. He understood the fact that they were hungry, and the heart of Christ was moved with compassion for them. He said, "No, get them to sit down. All there is in the company is 5,000 people, besides the women and children. Get them to sit down." When they were seated He took the five loaves and two fishes, blessed them, and gave to His disciples to give to the multitude.

Jesus taught the world compassion. Men might have compassion on the lovable and the beautiful; but Jesus taught the world to have compassion on the unholy and the ignorant. One day a sinful woman was brought to Him, and the people said, "According to our law, she should be stoned." According to the law there was nothing else for her, but the compassion of Jesus covered that soul. He said, "Go, and sin no more" (John 8:11).

I heard about a widow who lived in the country and was laboring for small wages. She had one daughter, and her great ambition was to be able to educate her daughter. She had toiled and worked and invested her money in liberty bonds to hold for the education of her daughter. She came down from one of the country towns to Spokane to make a few purchases necessary for the girl's new life at school. As she stood at one of the counters in a store, she turned her back for a moment, and soon discovered that the little treasure was gone. The savings of a whole life, the struggles of a mother's heart, gone! The endeavor to gratify the one big love of her soul in the education of her daughter was wiped out.

In spite of the assistance of the officials of the store, she was unable to find any trace of her money. At last she sat down and wept bitterly. A lady, the widow of a banker, who saw her told her to come up on the balcony with her and sit down. Another lady joined them, and the banker's widow said, "Now, come, we are going to sit down together and believe God on behalf of this soul. We are going to believe that God will move the soul of the person who took that money until his soul sees it as this mother sees it." They sat down together and prayed for that person. The mother returned to the country and in the mail following her came a letter with the money accompanied by a note saying, "I couldn't keep it; forgive me, and may God forgive me."

THE DIVINE SECRET

Compassion reaches further than law, further than demands of judges. Compassion reaches to the heart of life, to the secret of our being. The compassion of Jesus was the divine secret that made Him lovable. Religious people are exacting; good people are exacting; but good folk have to learn to exercise compassion just as others do.

We remember the incident with the disciples and the Samaritans. The Samaritans did not want Jesus and His disciples to come. They said, "We have heard strange stories, how this thing happened, and how that thing happened. How a great number of swine were drowned." They had heard about the pigs, but they probably had never heard how the widow's son was raised from the dead, or how the water had turned to wine. The disciples loved the Lord; they were exercising His power, they were ministering to the sick, they were endeavoring to alleviate the sufferings of the world. But still that sense of insult was so overpowering that they said, "Master, shall we call down fire from heaven to consume them?" How easy it is for us to feel the righteousness of the issue rather than the compassion of the Son of God. There is no limit to the compassion of Jesus.

Two blind men were crying by the wayside, calling on the Lord to have mercy on them. He stopped and asked what they wanted. They answered, "Lord, that our eyes may be opened" (Matt. 20:33). And He healed them. If you want the real explanation for His saving men out of their sins and sicknesses, it is in the love of His soul, that divine compassion of God, and His desire to help men out of their sorrows and back to God.

Jesus' example on the cross is set forever as the very acme, the very soul of the compassion of God through Christ. After the Roman soldiers had pierced His hands and feet, with His last breath He prayed to God, "Father, forgive them for they know not what they do." When a man is able to look upon His own murderers and speak such words as these, surely it shows that he speaks beyond that which the human heart is capable of giving, and is speaking only that which the soul of God can give.

How long should we endure the misunderstanding of friends without rebuff? If we consider these things, we see that He endured all the way. Unto the very end, and also in the very end, He was blessed by God. He was triumphant. The ignorant may crucify you and trample over the loveliest things of your soul, as they bruised the soul of Jesus. But you too can be triumphant.

ENDURING COMPASSION

In the divine fullness of the heart of God in Christ is the revelation of a divine conception that alone endures, even unto death, and through which the nature and love of God is revealed to a dying world. When Jesus was trying to give us balance in this life of God, He gave us the beautiful parable of the Good Samaritan. "A certain man went down from Jerusalem to Jericho, and fell among thieves, which stripped him of his raiment, and wounded him, and departed, leaving him half dead. And by chance there came down a certain priest that way" (Luke 10:30, 31).

One would have expected compassion of a priest, but when he saw him, he passed by on the other side. Then the Levite, the holy man of the people, came down and looked upon him. But he, too, passed by on the other side. The poor Samaritan, a dog in the mind of the Jew, "when he saw him, he had compassion on him, and went to him, and bound up his wounds, pouring in oil and wine, and set him on his own beast, and brought him to an inn, and took care of him. And on the morrow when he departed, he took out two pence, and gave them to the host, and said unto him, Take care of him; and whatsoever thou spendest more, when I come again, I will repay thee" (Luke 10:33-35). He did not do the best thing, but he did the best thing he knew, and Christ commended it.

How often have you had the loveliest things of your soul trampled upon? Perhaps not by some drunken person, but by one nearest to your heart, by the one who ought to have understood more than any other.

And do you not see the manner in which we wound the soul of Jesus continuously through our lack of holy compassion? There is something a man has never divined, and probably never will be able to divine—that subtle something in the nature that can be touched and moved by divine compassion. It tears down the bars of our lives and lets the divine love of God flow through our souls.

How often we have stood or knelt by the side of the dying and disease-smitten, and have waited and prayed, ineffectively, until within our heart something melted, something dissolved, and something richer than tears came from our souls. And by the grace of God we saw the answer to our prayers before our eyes.

The compassion of Jesus was illustrated when He broke up a funeral procession one day as He passed through the little city of Nain (Luke 7:11-17). When Jesus looked on that procession, something broke loose in His soul. He was moved with compassion as He saw the dead boy's mother, a widow, grieving for her only son. He stepped up to the bier and said, "Young man, I say unto thee, Arise."

The sorrows of others moved the soul of Jesus and touched His heart. Lazarus, His friend, died, and four days later the Lord went to him (John 11:1-44). Hearing that Jesus was approaching the village, one sister came to meet Him. She said to Him, "Lord, if thou hadst been here, my brother would not have died." The other sister poured out her heart to Him in a similar manner. As Jesus stood by the grave of His friend, He wept. Compassion stirred His soul. He said, "God, I thank thee that thou hearest me always." Then He cried with a loud voice, "Lazarus, come forth." And he that was dead came forth.

HEALING COMPASSION

Once in South Africa we were praying for a sick lady, for a time without result. Then I said, "I will take my sister and go pray for her." We prayed again, and there was no victory. A day or two afterwards my sister and I were in the city in one of the large department stores. As we stood there the Spirit of the Lord said to me, "Go to her now." I said to my sister, "As soon as you are through, we will go over and pray for that sick lady."

We went, and I watched her writhe in pain and agony until I put my arms about her and cuddled her head close to my heart. Soon something broke loose in my soul, and then in one moment (I hadn't even started to pray yet) she was lifted out of her agony and suffering. A divine flood moved her, and I knew she was healed. I laid her down on the bed, took my sister's arm, and we went away praising God.

I knew a man in South Africa who was an ardent Methodist. He had ten sons, all Methodist preachers, and three beautiful daughters who were holy women. This family was one of the most wonderful families I have ever known. The old father had been stricken with disease, and the agony of his suffering was so great that the only way to relieve him was to drug him into insensibility. As the years passed he became a morphine addict. He told me that he smoked 24 cigars, drank two quarts of whiskey, and used a tremendous quantity of morphine every day. The old man, 73 years old, was drugged into senselessness most of the time.

I prayed with him unceasingly for sixteen hours without result. William Duggin, one of my ministers, hearing of the situation, came to my assistance. He stood over the old gentleman and prayed for him in the power of God, but somehow there was no answer. I watched that man in convulsions until his daughters begged me to let them give him a little morphine and die senseless, rather than to let him suffer longer. I said, "No. I have had your pledge and his, too, that life or death, we are going to fight this battle through."

Presently as I stood there watching the awful convulsions, the Scripture came to my mind, "Himself took our infirmities" (Matt. 8:17). I reached out and got hold of him and held him as in a grip of iron. A compassion that is too deep for any form of expression we know broke forth in my soul; and in a single moment I saw him lie still, healed by God's power. Many a day after that I have walked with him over his three vast estates, on which there were 50,000 orange trees and 50,000 lemon trees. As we walked the old man told me of his love for God and of the richness of His presence, and I have my reward.

If the church ever succeeds in doing that which God purposes we should do, it can only be when we enter into that divine compassion of the Son of God.

CHAPTER 8

FELLOWSHIP WITH GOD

There is one word in the gospel that is the great inclusive word, comprehending all that God Almighty can accomplish in a human life. That word is **salvation.**

In our modern methods of subdiving the varied Christian experiences, we are in the habit of speaking of salvation in a very limited sense in comparison to the broad sense in which the word is used in Scripture.

I like to think of it as Jesus used it, the all-inclusive word. The one great big word of God that comprehends all that He can accomplish in a man's life forever, from the time He finds him as a sinner until the day Jesus Christ presents him to the Father, "holy and unblameable and unreprovable" in the sight of God. Until that day when with our Lord and Saviour Jesus Christ, we shall be acknowledged at the throne of God as heirs and joint-heirs with Him, and be given our place and part in the government of God's great kingdom.

There is much in a man's life besides "being good," if he is to fulfill his place in the world. God's first purpose is to make man good by removing the consciousness of sin from his soul, in order that he may grow up into God, and fulfill the great plan that God has in store for him, becoming a Son of God in mind, nature, power, and capacity to bless.

Christianity is different from every other religion in the world. Every other religion except Christianity has no need of a body or resurrection. Existence after death is purely a spirit existence. But not so with Christianity. Christianity has necessity for a resurrection. The reason for the resurrection is that the kingdom of Christ is not to be in heaven entirely. It is to be in this world. And the Lord and Saviour Jesus Christ is to rule in this world. Consequently, while we live in this world we will need a body like our Lord's—capable of existence here, and capable of existence over there.

The Word of God speaks of "the days of heaven upon the earth," when the conditions now prevalent exclusively in heaven are transferred to earth, and earth and heaven become one. These are "the days of heaven upon the earth." That is the kingdom of our Lord and Saviour Jesus Christ.

I imagine there will be railroads and cities in the kingdom, and there will be government in the kingdom. There will be a necessity for men grown up in God to take places of responsibility in the kingdom. If Jesus were to come into this audience tonight and ask for one hundred men who were capable of taking the affairs of Chicago in their hands tomorrow, perhaps not very many would qualify. Perhaps our capacity would be somewhat limited. Would He find us without capacity to operate its affairs successfully? Perhaps we would disappoint our Lord, and we would be very sad indeed.

The purpose of Jesus is not only to save men from their sins, but by the grace of God to begin in the souls of men that marvelous development in the nature and mind and understanding of God our Father, until by the grace of God we are able to take our place and our part in the kingdom of Jesus Christ and bear our share of responsibility.

PASSION FOR COMPANIONSHIP

I lived in South Africa as a missionary for some years, and among the craving passions of my soul that developed was a longing to get in contact with men of my own race and type of mind who understand the things that were moving my soul and who could comprehend the things I talked about.

When I returned to America I visited Brother Fockler in Milwaukee, and we talked nearly all night every night for a week. I just wanted to talk and listen. He could talk about the things my heart was longing to hear. Then I came to Chicago, and poor Brother Sinclair was nearly worn out, for I was so hungry for fellowship. There was a passion in my heart to hear his words and assimilate his thought, and to speak out understandingly. My soul longed to hear of the blessing of God and see another point of view. For almost a year we traveled from city to city as God led, contacting this soul and that soul, until that longing was satisfied, and I felt I could settle down in my own work again.

But you say, "There were lots of people in Africa that were good." Surely. We saw many thousands of saved native people, a multitude of them baptized in the Holy Ghost; they were a wonderful people. Notwithstanding their goodness, they had not been educated in the lines of thought that interested me. They could talk about God, but there were wonderful interests in the world of which they knew nothing, and my heart longed to be able to talk of these things. They were spiritual babies; they were intellectual babies. My heart was longing for companionship on my own plane of life.

If God had to exist forever and forever without companionship, the passion in the soul of God would remain unsatisfied. Man came into being because of a necessity in the soul of God. Children are born because of a necessity in the soul of the parents. It is the cry of the real father and the real mother. It is planted there from the heart of God Himself. Every true man wants to be a father, and every true woman a mother. They want to see their own offspring develop to manhood and womanhood and see themselves reproduced and perpetuated in the world.

God is perpetuating Himself in the soul of the Christian. God's heart is being satisfied in you and in me, because by the grace of God He expects us to grow up and out of our little environment and become sons of God and be able to have companionship with our Father. And He will tell us His purpose; He will reveal His wonderful plans of the future and we will be able to take part in the great enterprises of God forever.

The purpose of the Lord and Saviour was not only to redeem us out of filth and sin, but that we should grow up into manhood and womanhood in God, take our place in the world, and accomplish the thing God intended us to accomplish and fellowship with Him on His plane of understanding.

You are just as necessary to God in His plan for the salvation of mankind as God is necessary to you. This statement is so important I want to repeat it. Christians are just as necessary to Almighty God in order to accomplish His purpose in the world as God is necessary to the Christian. Without God we would not be saved. Without God we could not live. Without God we would never reach a maturity in Him. Without man God would have no medium through which He could express Himself to the world, by which He could minister the Spirit of the living God to the world.

That was the reason God had to send His own Son, Jesus Christ, there being no other competent to take His place. God "wondered that there was no man." He "marvelled that there was no intercessor," so His own right arm brought salvation, and His strength upheld Him.

Jesus was the first human body through which God revealed Himself to the world. After He returned to glory, He undertook to bring into being a new body. Not a lesser body, nor a weaker body, but a body greater than the body of Jesus, a power greater than the power of Jesus. That is the meaning of the words of Jesus: "Greater works than these shall he do; because I go unto my Father."

Unless Jesus Christ was the possessor of a divine secret, a secret that others did not understand, such words as these would be words of madness. But because Jesus understood the secret of returning to the Father, understood the secret of the Father's promise, understood what the possession of the Father's promise would mean to Him, and the world, He was able to say those marvelous words, ". . . Greater works than these shall he do; because I go unto my Father" (John 14:12).

We have treated the precious Spirit of God as though He is a method of providing a means of spiritual entertainment for our souls. God's purpose is far mightier than that. God's purpose is that our spirit be tuned to heaven, our heart capable of hearing and realizing the songs of glory, appreciating companionship with God and feeling flames of His divine love, expressing and revealing it to the hungry world that knows not God.

In the old days when I was in Africa I would walk into the native meetings where I did not understand the language, and listen to the preacher for an hour. I did not understand a word he said, but my soul was blessed by the presence of the Spirit of God.

As bishop of the church I went from place to place holding conferences among white and native people. In many of them people would speak either English or Dutch. But I was just as much blessed when a Dutchman spoke, even though I did not understand him, as when an Englishman spoke, because the thing that blessed my soul was the living Spirit of God. Perhaps I had heard better words than his, perhaps clearer explanation of the Scriptures than he could give, but I was blessed by the presence of God. The thing that the individual was ministering to my soul was the living Spirit of God.

The ministry of the Christian is a ministry of the Spirit. If the Christian cannot minister the Spirit of God in the true sense, he is not a Christian. If he has not the Spirit to minister in the real sense, he has nothing to minister. Other men have intellectuality, but the Christian is supposed to be the possessor of the Spirit. He possesses something that no other man in the whole world possesses; that is, the Spirit of the living God.

MORE THAN PSYCHOLOGICAL INFLUENCES

The Spirit of God at work in a man goes thousands of miles beyond psychological influence. If you want a clear distinction between psychological religions, as they are called, or mental science, you can see it in a minute. The real Christian ministers the real Spirit of God, the substance of His being. There should never be any misunderstanding along these lines.

A minister of Jesus Christ is as far removed from the realm of psychological influence as heaven is from the earth. He ministers God Himself into the very spirits and souls and bodies of men. That is the reason a Christian throws down the bars of his nature and invites God to come in and take possession of his being. The incoming of God into our body, into our soul, into our spirit accomplishes marvelous things in the nature of man.

A man came to me one day and said, "I am almost ashamed to call myself a man, because I have simply indulged the animal of my nature so that I am more a beast than a man. You say, 'Why don't you quit such a life?' I have not the strength of will to do so. Unless something takes place that will deliver me from this condition, I do not know what I will do."

I tried to show him what the gospel of Jesus Christ was. I tried to show him that through living in the animal state, surrounding himself with beastly suggestion, and contacting the spirit of bestiality everywhere that that element had taken possession of him so that it dominated his nature. I said, "My son, if the gospel means anything it means there shall be a transference of nature. Instead of this living hell that is present in your being, the living, holy God should flow into your life and cast the devil out, dispossess the beast, and reign in your members."

We knelt to pray, and today he came back with tears in his eyes and said, "Mr. Lake, I feel I can shake hands with you now. I am a beast no more. I am a man."

Recently a dear woman was present in our meeting with a tumor that her physicians had believed to be an unborn child until the tumor became larger than a normal unborn child. The physicians had been fooled by a movement which they considered similar to life movement. They believed the woman would become a mother, until the normal time of pregnancy had long passed. She came with her nurse to the healing rooms and told me her symptoms. She was the first one to be prayed for at the close of the service. The next day she returned and said, "Mr. Lake, I want you to see me. I have my corset on. I am perfectly normal. When I went to bed I was not aware that anything had taken place, except that the choking had ceased and I felt comfortable, but I was not aware of any decreasing in my size. When I awoke this morning I was perfectly normal."

I said, "How did the tumor disappear? Was it in the form of a liquid?" She said, "No, nothing came from my person."

Where did a great tumor like that go? What happened to it? The living Spirit of God absolutely dematerialized the tumor and the process was accomplished in one night while the woman slept. That is one of God's methods of surgical operations, isn't it?

The Spirit of God took possession of that dear soul's body. That tumor became filled with the Spirit of God, and the effect of the Spirit of God in that tumor was so mighty, so powerful, that the Spirit of God dissolved it.

That is the secret of the ministry of Jesus Christ. That is the secret of the ministry of Christianity. The real Christian who lives in union with the living God and possesses His Spirit has a ministry that no other man in all the world possesses. The real Christian here has a revelation of Jesus Christ and His power to save that no other human in all the world possesses. Why? He is full and experiences in his own soul the dissolving power of the Spirit of God that takes sin out of his life and makes him a free man in Christ Jesus.

DELIVERANCE FROM THE DEMON OF ALCOHOL

One day a woman called me over the telephone and said, "I have a young friend who is a drunkard, and the habit has such power over him that he will go to any excess to obtain it. Dry state or no dry state, he has to have it. He is an intelligent fellow. He wants to be free. We have invited him to my home for prayer, and he is here now. I want you to join me in prayer for him."

I said, "All right, but first you call one of your neighbors to join you in prayer for this man; then when you are ready call me on the phone, and Mr. Westwood and Mrs. Petersen and I will join you in prayer."

She called me in a little while and we united our hearts in prayer for the young man, who was on the other side of the city. About twenty minutes later he rose from his knees and with tears in his eyes he took the woman by the hand and said, "I know when something has taken place within me . . ." The appetite had disappeared. That is the ministry of the Spirit, the ministry of God to man.

Isn't it a marvelous thing that God has ordained an arrangement whereby man becomes God's own co-partner and co-laborer in the ministry of the Spirit? "The church which is His body." Just as Jesus Christ was the human body through which the living Spirit was ministered to mankind, so God has arranged that the living church, not the dead member, alive with the Spirit of the living God, should minister that quickening life to another, and thereby become a copartner, a co-laborer together with God.

CHAPTER 9

THE SECRET OF MIRACLES

I want to read a few words from the second chapter of Hebrews as a basis for my thought. God says of man:

> "But one in a certain place testified, saying, What is man, that thou art mindful of him? or the son of man, that thou visitest him? Thou madest him a little lower than the angels; thou crownedst him with glory and honour and didst set him over the works of thy hands: Thou hast put all things in subjection under his feet. For in that he put all in subjection under him, he left nothing that is not put under him. But now we see not yet all things put under him" (Heb. 2:6-8).

Now I am going to read what I believe to be the most startling statement in the Word of God, and doubly startling because Jesus Himself said it. You and I are ready to conceive no doubt that by the marvelous processes revealed in the Word of God and by His Holy Spirit, God has an amazing purpose for man, and that Jesus Christ in very truth has made provision for man's salvation and man's exaltation to the very throne of God.

In the tenth chapter of John, Jesus was preaching and He got along nicely until He made this statement:

> "Then the Jews took up stones again to stone him. Jesus answered them, Many good works have I shewed you from my Father; for which of

those works do ye stone me? The Jews answered him, saying, For a good work we stone thee not; but for blasphemy; and because that thou, being a man, makest thyself God. Jesus answered them, Is it not written in your law, I said, Ye are gods? If he called them gods, unto whom the word of God came, and the scripture cannot be broken; Say ye of him, whom the Father hath sanctified, and sent into the world, Thou blasphemest; because I said, I am the Son of God?" (John 10:31-36).

The startling thing in that statement is not that Jesus said it to those who had definitely accepted Him as their Lord and Saviour, and who had experienced the power of His salvation. But these words were spoken to those who had not accepted Him, and who apparently were still living in sin and prejudice against Christ. To such Jesus said: "Ye are gods." That reveals the divine potential in man. If you are going to quarrel with anyone about that statement, you will have to quarrel with the Lord. Jesus said, "Ye are gods." And the Scripture in Heb. 2:7, 8, adds, "And didst set him over the works of thy hands: Thou hast put all things in subjection under his feet."

In the beginning of creation the Lord said: "Adam, I give you dominion over the fish of the sea, over the beasts of the field, and over the fowls of the air." And the original man, clothed in the likeness of Christ, was ruler in earth and sea and sky.

I never could imagine that when Adam wanted the cows, he went out with a club and a dog to get them. There was a dominion in his spirit that the animal kingdom recognized, that the birds knew and the fish understood. Man was God's king— God's king upon earth. And if we want tangible evidence of the wreckage that sin made in the world, we do not have to go further than our own selves to discover that when the Christ dominion is gone, it is the evidence of the deepest degeneration. A king without a kingdom, a king without kingliness of character, a king robbed of his power.

Man had fallen from his high place. Man had fallen from his glorious position. He had lost his dominion. Indeed the ravages of sin have been such that man in his spiritual capacity, in his moral nature, in his capacity for the exercise of power, has become greatly weakened. Weakened to the degree that instead of ruling the animal world, the animal nature rules him. The elements rule him, control him. Sin chokes the virtue from his soul, and Satan laughs him to scorn.

Because of the weakened state of our physical being through sin, we have become subject to the varied laws of nature about us. We get in a draft and catch cold. We develop pneumonia. The waves toss us about. The terrors of life frighten us, all of which through Jesus Christ was meant to be reversed. And in Christ it is reversed. Through Christ's indwelling, man is restored to his former state.

Real salvation is not mere forgiveness of sins or the mere cleansing of the heart from sin's power, or the nominal baptism in the Holy Ghost. Christ's salvation is intended to bring again into the nature of man that which was lost through sin. Once again through the divine operation of the Spirit of God, ministered to our hearts by Jesus Christ, His overcoming Son, the divine Spirit that rules in the soul of Jesus should rule in the nature of man. Thus once more, by the grace of God, man takes his place before God in the state and status in which God created him in the beginning—a son of God.

And lest we be discouraged in observing that thus far we have not attained, Paul calls our attention to the fact in Hebrews 2:8 that though "we see not yet all things put under him" (man), we see Jesus, the one overcomer, who entered again into the divine fullness of God's estate for man, become to man forever God's divine inspiration and pattern of a real man and son of God.

My heart is longing these days, since God commenced to teach me of His wonderful purpose by the Spirit, that you and I in very truth begin to lift our heads knowing that "our redemption draweth nigh."

PURPOSE OF GOD AFTER THE RAPTURE

Beloved, the eventual purpose of Christians and Christianity (for Christianity has an eventual purpose in this world) is not that we be translated to go off floating in the heavens. The rapture is only an incident. The rapture is at the best a very short period. That period in our experience will correspond to the forty days in which Jesus took the disciples after the Resurrection into the mountains of Galilee. There He had them alone where He could teach them the higher things of God that had been evolved in His soul through His entrance and experience in the regions of death— the divine overcoming and liberation of those held by its chains, and the overcoming and mastery of death itself. So that when He came forth from the grave, the great soul of the Son of God in divine passion was waiting for the opportunity to pour it out, to give the balm of it and the soul of it to His disciples.

So the first time they came together He breathed on them and said, "Receive ye the Holy Ghost." He was breathing into them the new dominion born in His soul through His victory over death and hell.

SIN ROBS MAN OF HIS DOMINION

Sin always has the same reaction in a man's life. Sin produces fear. It is the consciousness of guilt, the consciousness of failure—the product of fear.

Fear causes the spirit of man to lose its sense of dominion. It causes the mind of man to become subjective. It causes the person of man to become subservient. When Christ ceases to reign, and the consciousness of dominion is gone from the spirit of man, his whole attitude toward life is changed. Instead of being God's prince, ruling by the dominion of Christ, his nature is made subjective and subservient to the conditions about him.

But Christ, coming into a man's life by the Spirit, exalts His nature into divine dominion. The rulership of God and the power of Christ in his heart makes him once again God's prince and king in the world.

If you could examine the very structure of the mind you would observe that when a man's heart is filled with fear, instead of being dominant, instantly he is made subjective. His head drops, his face grows pale, his whole demeanor is changed. And if you could examine the pores of his flesh during such a time, you would see a reverse action. He is drawing to himself, absorbing into himself, the spirit around him—whether that spirit be disease or mental torment, or whatever the condition; he is taking the curse to himself.

WHEN FAITH COMES—FEAR IS BANISHED

But instantly when fear is banished and faith from God comes, a man's whole nature is changed by the power of its indwelling. Instantly the Spirit is dominant, and his mind is positive. His person repels and rejects every form of darkness and disease by the outflow and emanation of the Spirit of God.

It is my conviction that when Satan came to the Lord Jesus Christ, he talked to Him from a respectful distance. In Satan's complaint to God concerning Job he says: "Hast not thou made an hedge about him, and about his house, and about all that he hath on every side?" (Job 1:10). God was not standing out with a gun to keep the serpent from stealing his camels. But God had established in the soul of Job the dominion of God. He was God's prince, God's king, and as long as that condition of dominion remained in his soul, no power of darkness could touch him. Not even the things he possessed were in danger. He was God's king.

But right away when that condition changed, Job commenced to scratch himself with an old piece of pottery; his spirit was drooping, his mind was subjective, and his body was covered with boils. His spirit could not rise to that high place in God until once again God came and comforted him by His Word and strengthened him by the mightiest sermon that was ever preached to a human soul. Under its magic power Job's spirit lifted into God again. He was master, until at the wonder of it all he forgot himself and prayed for his friends and his deliverance came.

WHAT DID JESUS MEAN, "YE ARE GODS"?

On what ground did Jesus reason when He said to those sinful Jews: "I said, ye are gods . . . and the scripture cannot be broken" (John 10:34, 35)? This takes us back to the creation of man when God breathed into him the breath of life, and the living Spirit of the Father and of the Son and of the Holy Ghost came into his life and nature, when dominion over sin and dominion over sickness was native in the soul of man.

God's great purpose through Jesus Christ is not that we should float off in the air and sing forever and ever, it is in what follows the rapture. The objective of Christianity is the kingdom of the Lord and Saviour Jesus Christ in this world. When this world is changed by the power of God, when earth becomes a part of heaven, and the same conditions that now prevail in heaven are here in the world, won't it be wonderful?

But somebody will have to go out and clean up the world. There will be something for you to do in the kingdom. You will not always be floating around in the air and singing, "Hallelujah!" When we return with Jesus to enjoy His kingdom, we will have our part to do. Earth is to become a part of heaven. There will always be "days of heaven on the earth."

That explains why Christianity is different from every other form of religion. Christianity provides a resurrection because Christianity has need of a resurrection. No other religion has any need for a resurrection. With them existence is purely in the spirit. The individual has no body, has no use for a body, because he has no place where a body will be valuable. But bless God! When earth becomes a part of heaven, Christianity has need of a body, a risen God, a resurrected body, a glorified body.

Now, somebody is wondering what all that has to do with the secret of miracles. Just this: God has to disabuse the mind of man of that which the devil has promulgated from time immemorial, and particularly through the church—that man is a vile worm without value and that hell was created for his particular reception. But God never created hell for man. Man has created his own hell. It is a fit place for all your cancers and tumors and diseases and cursed sicknesses.

But God has a purpose for you, and God has a purpose for me. God's exalted purpose for us is to take us into fellowship with the Lord and Saviour Jesus Christ, to make us brothers in our Lord. He is our elder brother. He pushes us forward, encourages our soul, says to us when we are discouraged, "Go on, you can win. I am at your back."

As the prodigal who was in the enemy's territory had to come to himself, so man has to find himself. Man discovers Christ's purpose for him; he discovers why Jesus died. He discovers the exalted purpose that Christ had in mind for every man, for the holy day when by the grace of God the sons of God will put the crown of glory on the head of Jesus Christ and the world will proclaim Him King of kings and Lord of lords.

LIFT UP YOUR HEADS

Beloved, lift up your heads. If there are any people on earth who ought to walk with uplifted heads and uplifted hearts, surely it is the men and women who claim to be anointed of the Holy Ghost. I am eager that somehow God will help us to that divine dignity, that heavenly power and purity, that divine character and holy nature that God revealed through Jesus Christ as our inheritance.

Rudyard Kipling wrote these beautiful lines in trying to reveal this truth:

"And oft there cometh the wise Lord God,
Master of every trade,
And he tells them tales of his daily toils,
And of Edens, newly made,
And they rise to their feet as He passeth by,
Gentlemen, unafraid."

That is my conception of Christ's salvation. That is what my heart reads in this blessed Word of God. That is the way my spirit interprets the precious Spirit of Jesus Christ. That is the revelation that Jesus brought from heaven for a world that is down. He can reveal to your soul the God-possibility and quality of your nature, and show you that instead of being in the likeness of Christ as He intended you to be, you have sold yourself out to the world, the flesh and the devil, and become debased in your nature. Rise, beloved, rise up to victory!

A COMPLETE COMMITTAL OF SPIRIT, SOUL AND BODY TO GOD

Once in my life I was very ill, ill unto death. I had reasoned in my heart that unless God came my time was short. Long before, I had put myself in God's hands and committed my spirit, soul, and body to Him. When I gave myself to God, I gave Him my body as well as my soul and my spirit, and that meant that I would trust God and Him only, and I would die before I would violate my covenant with God.

So I said, "If I have to die, I will die like a man and like a Christian." And He lifted me! You know, there used to be beautiful Christian deathbeds. That was before the days of narcotics and the hypodermic needle. There are few Christian deaths these days. They die like animals. They cannot talk to their families, let alone God.

Christian deathbeds are largely a thing of the past. The glory of God came to the old saints, and they waited in anticipation for the hour when their spirits were liberated. When heaven was near, their spiritual senses were keener, their perceptive powers clarified. They told of God and heaven and waiting angels.

When I was a boy of 16, I was invited to the bedside of a young lady who was dying. When I got there a group of young people had already gathered. We knew nothing of praying for healing. We had come at the woman's request. She wanted to tell us of the glories of God that had come to her dying vision, and she could not pass on until she had shared her vision. She desired it to inspire our hearts to be true. After I left that room I walked with a soft tread for many days. I was walking in a new presence, a new realization, a consciousness that God was not so far away, and heaven was just as close as Jesus Christ is to the Christian hearts.

THE SECRET OF MIRACLES

It is that purpose of God that is the whole key to the secret of miracles. It is because your soul and the soul of the Son of God cease to be two souls any longer, and you become one. His life is breathed into you. His nature is burned into you, the fire of His holy soul is flaming in you and flashing through you. His dominion is not a word but a fact in your soul.

Jesus Christ on the Mount of Transfiguration is God's eternal pattern of how much man may become absorbed in and reflect and reveal God. When Jesus was transfigured before His disciples, His clothes became white and glistening. His face shone as the light. There is a touch here that I praise God for. The Word says the transfiguration took place while He prayed. While He was praying, He was transfigured. It reveals the power of prayer.

It reveals that man is the most divine instrument in all God's creation for the revelation of God. That living Spirit of God energizes him, leaps from him as the lightning. Dear brother, dear sister, let me encourage your heart. Everything in the world of God that ever was possible to the Lord Jesus Christ is likewise possible to the Christian. He purposed by God's grace to lift us up until we stand together on God's plane, Christ-conquerors, Christ-revealers.

Yes, the Lord found us. We were in sickness and in shame, and by the grace of God He healed us from our sicknesses and cleansed us from our sins. Then He came and indwelt heart and life. He lives in us and undertakes to transform our nature and our character, our very person and being—so that our spirit and soul, body and blood may become spirit of His Spirit, soul of His soul, flesh of His flesh, bone of His bone, and blood of His blood.

CHAPTER 10

THE HABITATION OF GOD

God has been seeking a habitation for a long time. God found a habitation in Jesus Christ and He became the dwelling place of God. Christ's purpose for the world was that man, like Himself, should become the dwelling place of God. It was purposed that mankind should be as holy and desirable a dwelling place of God as was Jesus Himself.

The purpose of the gospel was that through Jesus Christ, God's Son, many sons should be begotten of God. Christ's undertaking was to save men from their sins and transform them into sons of God like Himself. That is the purpose and work of our Lord and Saviour Jesus Christ.

In I Corinthians 15 we read of the consummation of His purpose—that is, the conclusion of that purpose when Jesus, having subjected all things unto Himself, is Himself also subjected unto the Father that God may be all in all. Not a dissenting voice, not a rebellious heart. The will of God has been received, and as a result there is no longer a necessity for a Saviour; Jesus Christ in His capacity of Saviour of the world has completed His mission.

In the great struggle we see about us and the struggle we recognize in our nature, we are sometimes prone to feel that there cannot possibly be a time of ultimate and final victory of the Lord

Jesus Christ in the souls of men. However, the Word of God portrays a time and conception of the purpose of Jesus Christ when the world, being redeemed unto Christ, no longer needs the redeeming merit of the Saviour.

PAUL SEES CHRIST'S PURPOSE

I have always regarded the first and second chapters of Ephesians as two of the most remarkable in the entire Word of God. Perhaps no soul ever envisioned the real purpose of God and portrayed it in words with more clearness than did Paul in these two chapters.

In the first chapter he begins by showing us that Jesus fulfilled the purpose of the Father, that as a reward for His consecration to the will of God, His death, resurrection, ascension and glorification, the power of God ruled in His nature, and He was in very truth the Son of God to whom was committed all authority and all power. Principalities and powers, Paul says, were subject unto Him.

Then in the second chapter he begins to make this truth applicable to our own heart, and he undertakes to show us that just as Jesus Christ was dead and in the grave—so mankind, possessed and dominated by the power of sin and selfishness has become "dead in sin;" that is, senseless to the Spirit of God. And as Jesus was raised from the dead, so He has purposed to lift the veil or cloud, the obsession or possession of sin, and cleanse the nature of man and unify him with God.

When he reaches this climax he puts it in this terse form: ". . . to make in himself of twain one new man, so making peace" (Eph. 2:15). He shows us that the ultimate and final peace that comes to the soul of man comes as the result of a divine union having taken place between Jesus Christ and the Christian soul, and there is no longer any worry or discussion over commandments or ordinances. The soul has risen above them. It has risen out of the region of commandments and laws into a government of love. The soul joined to Christ in His divine affection, the spirit of man entering into Christ, the spirit of Christ entering into man, causing such a transformation that the man becomes a new creature. All his impulses have changed; the ruling of his human nature ceases and finally he is a son of God.

That is the wonder of the cleansing power and cross of Christ in the nature of man. The wonder is that Jesus purposed to make your heart and mine just as sweet and lovely and pure and holy as His own. That is the reason He can accept the Christian as His bride. Who could imagine Christ accepting Christians who are polluted, defiled, of a lower state of purity or holiness than Himself?

If you have felt that you have been a sinner "above all that have dwelt in Jerusalem," be assured that the cleansing power of Jesus Christ is equal to your need, and the thoroughness of His Spirit's working in you can make you a king and prince, lovely and beautiful, pure of heart and life, like unto Himself.

The aspiration of every teacher is to bring his student to his own level of understanding. The triumph of every teacher is to inspire within the student the possibility of even surpassing the teacher in his search for knowledge and truth. Could we expect of Jesus a lesser purpose than that which we recognize in teachers everywhere? If Jesus is a Redeemer, unto what is He to redeem us? What is the ideal? What is the standard to which Christ purposes to bring us? Is the standard less than that which He holds Himself? If so, it would be unworthy of the Son of God. He would not be giving to us the best He has.

The Word of God stands clear in one respect—that "the blood of Jesus Christ his Son cleanseth us from all sin" (I John 1:7). Clean in our nature, thoroughly cleansed by His grace, every atom and fiber of the spirit, soul and body of man made sweet and holy, like unto Jesus Himself.

THE PURPOSE OF CLEANSING

This marvelous cleansing by the Spirit and power of Jesus Christ is for a definite purpose; it is a definite preparation. When we make an elaborate preparation of any kind it is so that something may follow. So this preparation in holiness and righteousness and truth in the nature of man by Jesus Christ, the Word declares, is that there may be a fitting climax. The climax is that man may become the dwelling place of God.

God demands a holy temple through which His holiness may be revealed. Consequently, it becomes a matter of necessity to the Lord Jesus Christ that if He is to reveal Himself in a hundredfold measure through the church to the world, He must have the ability to cleanse the church and present her, as the Word portrays, "without spot or wrinkle or any such thing." She must be as pure as Jesus is pure, beautiful within, beautiful without. The scars and wrinkles must disappear. So Christ will receive the really Christ-cleansed church as His own virgin, the Bride.

THE WONDER OF HIS GRACE

The wonder of the grace of God is revealed in us, though we have sinned, though we have become polluted, though in our soul life we have practiced adultery with the spirit of the world until the nature of the world has entered into our nature and soiled it and made it unlike the nature of Jesus Christ. And the wonder of His grace is that He receives us, cleanses us, purifies us, saves us, and being thus redeemed and cleansed by the Spirit of

Christ, we stand sweet and holy and lovely in His presence, prepared to be His bride. One in which He can live, with whom He can fellowship, into whose nature He purposes now to come and abide.

If you will study with care the life of the apostles you will observe that there was a process that took place in their lives so thorough and complete that Jesus said to them prior to His departure, "Now ye are clean through the word that I have spoken unto you" (John 15:3).

They had arrived in soul cleansing at the place where, by the grace of God, they were prepared for the next experience and higher purpose of Jesus, which was that they might now receive the Holy Ghost. That the Spirit of Jesus Christ might come from heaven to abide in them and thus cause them to become the dwelling place of God.

The purpose of Christ was that not only the twelve, and the 120 upon whom the Holy Ghost came at Jerusalem and the church at Samaria, and the household of Cornelius, should be cleansed and receive the Holy Spirit, but also that every son of God should receive a like experience. The church at Samaria was different from the church at Jerusalem in that it was composed of the wandering heathen tribes, and it was different from the household of Cornelius, which were intelligent Romans. But they were all in common with all the race in that they became the habitation of God through the Spirit.

In all these instances we see that the purpose of God is not only to cleanse a man, but being cleansed to also empower him, to infill him, to indwell him by His own blessed Spirit. The Holy Spirit present in a holy temple reveals Himself through that person, just as He did through the Lord Jesus Christ.

THE SPIRIT OF JESUS

If we study the manner by which the Spirit of God revealed Himself through Jesus Christ, then we will have the pattern or example of how the Spirit of God reveals Himself through all believers.

The Spirit of God spoke through Him the word of love, the word that brought conviction, the word of power. Through His nature flowed a subtle something that no religionist but Himself and His followers possessed—the living Spirit of the living God, the anointing of the Holy Ghost, the one characteristic that makes Christianity a distinctive religion forever. It can never be identified with any other. So long as Christianity is dependent on the presence of the anointing of the Holy Ghost, it will remain distinctively one religion, that divine power and saving grace.

If you held the hand of Jesus tonight, do you suppose your spirit would be capable of searching His soul to know whether He was pure? No, but instinctively something in that purer Spirit would cause you to know it was your Lord.

Then suppose that the Spirit of Jesus searched our own, what would He discern? That is the question men are continuously compelled to ask of themselves. What would the Spirit of Jesus discern in me? Would He be drawn to us or would we repel Him because of our unholiness?

The Word of God lays blessed and splendid emphasis on the fact that we need the cleansing power of Jesus to make our spirit pure like His own. Then having cleansed us and sanctified us to Himself, the Holy Spirit comes to dwell in our nature and take up His eternal residence in us. Thus we become the habitation of God through the Spirit.

I sat one day on the platform of a great tabernacle in the presence of 10,000 people who had gathered to hear me preach. I had received a promise from God for that occasion as I lay in my bed the night before. The Spirit of the Lord had given me in His own words an outline of the history of man's nature from the creation to the redemption and empowering by the Spirit of God. But the anointing from heaven that would make possible the presentation of such an ideal and make it acceptable to the hearts of thousands who listened had not yet come.

As I sat there praying I was conscious of the Spirit upon me until my nature was overcome by it. I could hardly stay in my seat I was so eager for the moment when the preliminaries were finished so I could get a chance to deliver my message.

Such is the marvel of the nature of man united with Christ, when the abundant fullness of His holy nature may come to you and me when our temple has been prepared to receive Him. If you have been getting along with only a limited measure of blessing in your daily life, let me encourage you that the fountain will not be exhausted when your spirit is filled with the overflow.

GOD'S SPIRIT MULTIPLIED

The Spirit of God is like the bread that the disciples distributed to the multitude. It became filled with the Spirit of God; it multiplied in their hands. When they broke some off, there was more remaining than when they had begun. The Spirit of God is creative, generative, constructive, and the more you give the more you receive. There must be a great opening of the nature of man in order that he may be a large receiver, and the strangeness of it is that it depends upon whether we are large givers. It is a violation of every known law of man, but it is the common law of the Spirit. Why? Because the Spirit, unlike other things, is creative. He grows, He magnifies in your soul; He multiplies as you share Him with another.

Jesus laid down a perpetual law. "Give, and it shall be given unto you; good measure, pressed down, and shaken together, and running over, shall men give into your bosom. For with the same measure that ye mete withal it shall be measured to you again" (Luke 6:38).

In my experience of 25 years of healing ministry, I have known very few instances of a person's being healed when he approached me with such words as, "If I am healed, I will give the church so much." The reason is that the Spirit is not received on those terms. We are just entering into a knowledge of the law of Jesus Christ: "Give and it shall be given unto you."

Christ is seeking for the soul who will receive His love, and the real Christian who is seeking for the Christ will receive His love. Both are practicing the unalterable law of God, "Give, and it shall be given unto you."

Frequently we observe that sympathy becomes the door through which affection enters. I once asked a nurse what the hardest thing in a nurse's life was. She said, "If you remain a woman and do not become steeled in your nature and hardened in your affections, you will find it the most difficult thing to keep from permitting your affections to follow your sympathy."

And over and over as a law of life, a woman will nurse a man, and before she is through she will love him. Why? Because sympathy for him has opened the door of her nature and unconsciously it has flowed out in affection to him.

There is a thing that is dearer to God than anything else, and the only thing that is worthwhile. It is the same thing that is dear to every man. That is the affection of your heart.

Your son may rise to a place of eminence and respect in the world, and yet your soul may be disappointed. Why? Because the soul of the real father is seeking something besides that. He is seeking the affection of the son, and if he fails to receive that all the rest is worthless.

Christ is seeking the affection of mankind, the union of man's spirit with His, for without man's affection there can never be that deep union of the Spirit between God and man that makes possible a richness of life, made glorious by His indwelling. That is why the love of God is shown in the Word as the one supreme attraction to draw the soul of man in returned affection.

You can give the Lord your money, your property, your brain, and all the other things that are usually considered to be excellent; but if you withhold your affections from Him and give them to another, the Word says you are an adulterer.

So long as religion exists you will never be able to separate real religion from the emotions of the soul. The emotions will be an open door through which the Spirit finds access to your life. When you reduce religious life to a science, and take from it the warmth of Christ's affection, you have robbed it of its charm and its almighty power.

GOD IN MAN'S MIND, SPIRIT AND BODY

When we become the habitation of God and He lives in our mind, what will we do and what will we think? What will be the tenderness of our emotions, of our soul, what will be the depth of our feelings, what will be the growth of our capacity to love?

God lives in a man's spirit, the spirit of man reaching out into the boundless, touching the almightiness of God, discerning His nature, appropriating His power, securing His almightiness.

God lives in a man's flesh, giving off a vibration of God-life, God-power, God indwelling in his blood, God indwelling in his hands, God indwelling his bones and marrow—a habitation of God.

OTHER JOHN G. LAKE BOOKS

SERMONS ON DOMINION OVER DEMONS, DISEASE & DEATH
This volume, reprinted eight times, contains 15 powerful sermons on dominion by Dr. John G. Lake.
$1.50

THE NEW JOHN G. LAKE SERMONS
The second volume of Lake sermons contains seven faith-building messages by this powerful expositor.
$1.50

JOHN G. LAKE—APOSTLE TO AFRICA
After a long procession of sickness and death in his family, Dr. Lake was led into a ministry of divine healing. This book relates how God led him to Africa, and tells of the mighty revival that shook a whole nation for God.
$1.00

(Prices subject to change without notice)

Order books by title

CHRIST FOR THE NATIONS
BOX 24910 • DALLAS, TX 75224